Congregational Church Henniker (N.H.).

Proceedings of the One Hundred and Fifteenth Anniversary of the Congregational Church

Henniker, N.H., Saturday, June 7, 1884

Congregational Church Henniker (N.H.).

Proceedings of the One Hundred and Fifteenth Anniversary of the Congregational Church
Henniker, N.H., Saturday, June 7, 1884

ISBN/EAN: 9783337260309

Printed in Europe, USA, Canada, Australia, Japan

Cover: Foto ©ninafisch / pixelio.de

More available books at **www.hansebooks.com**

PROCEEDINGS

1769　　　　OF THE　　　　1884

ONE HUNDRED AND FIFTEENTH

ANNIVERSARY OF THE

CONGREGATIONAL CHURCH,

HENNIKER, N. H.,

SATURDAY, JUNE 7, 1884.

COMMENCING AT NINE A. M., AND HOLDING OVER THE SABBATH.

PRINTED BY VOTE OF THE CHURCH; REV. J. H. HOFFMAN, PASTOR.

BRISTOL, N. H.:
PRINTED BY R. W. MUSGROVE.
1884.

LETTER OF INVITATION.

Henniker, N. H., April, 1884.

Dear..

The "*Church of Christ*" of *Henniker*, of the Calvinistic Congregational order, sends hearty greeting, and hopes to welcome and entertain you at the one hundred and fifteenth (115th) Anniversary of its organization, on Saturday and Sunday, June 7th and 8th, 1884.

Appropriate Exercises by former and present members of the Church and Society will be in order.

Please invite, in behalf of the committee, any member or townsmen who once worshipped with us.

If you cannot be present, please make a communication to be read at the time mentioned. Pray that the Divine Spirit shall take the humble deeds of the Church and bless them to generations to come.

HORACE CHILDS,
S. W. CARTER,
LEVI S. CONNOR,
S. Q. A. NEWTON,
L. W. PEABODY,
J. H. HOFFMAN,
Committee.

OFFICERS OF THE DAY.

S. Q. A. NEWTON, President.

HARRIS W. CAMPBELL, Musical Director.

CARRIE L. MORSE, Organist.

ORDER OF EXERCISES.

MORNING.

1. ORGAN VOLUNTARY.
2. ANTHEM.—"Praise the Lord."
3. INVOCATION.   REV. E. H. HOUSE.
4. READING OF THE SCRIPTURES.   REV. GEO. W. SAVORY.
5. PRAYER.   REV. WILLIAM WOOD.
6. ADDRESS OF WELCOME.   BY THE PASTOR.
7. HYMN.—No. 708.
8. LETTERS FROM ABSENT MEMBERS.
9. POEM.   EDNA DEAN PROCTOR.
10. ADDRESS.—"The Church an Educator."
     HON. J. W. PATTERSON.
11. "THE CHOIRS AND CHORISTERS OF THE CHURCH."
     HON. OLIVER PILLSBURY.
12. ANTHEM. BENEDICTION.   REV. J. H. ROWELL.

COLLATION.

AFTERNOON.

1. ANNIVERSARY HYMN. Written for the day by
     REV. N. F. CARTER.
2. HISTORIC ADDRESS.   REV. J. M. R. EATON.
     (Pastor of the Church for seventeen years.)
3. HYMN.—No. 954.
4. REMINISCENCES.
     By former pastors and past and present members.
5. THE MISSION WORK OF THE CHURCH.
     REV. WILLIAM WOOD.
6. THE SABBATH-SCHOOL. Address to the Children.
     *REV. G. H. MORSS. (Former Pastor.)
   (The two latter parts were assigned for the Lord's Day.)
7. ANTHEM. "Jerusalem—My Happy Home."
8. BENEDICTION.

*Rev. G. H. Morse was detained by an accident. Mr. Nathan Sanborn and Hon. J. W. Patterson addressed the Sabbath-School.

ADDRESS OF WELCOME.

BY THE PASTOR.

CHRISTIAN SISTERS AND BROTHERS:—

The grateful acknowledgment of your presence here to-day is better done than said, yet with 115 years behind and you before me how can I resist the temptation to put our welcome into words.

By the provident hand of our God, whose blessing has been invoked, we gather to speak of the deeds of the church of Christ. We have in our letter of invitation asked you to "pray that the Divine Spirit shall take the humble deeds of the church and bless them to the generations to come." I am the commissioned welcomer of the day. Therefore with authority do I speak. We are glad to see you. A scene in Shakspeare represents Leontes opening his free arms and weeping his welcome forth. We shall try to suppress our tears until you have gone except the quantity of your attendance shall compel us to adopt the 83rd line of the 15th book of the Odyssey, which reads thus:—

"Welcome the coming but speed the going guest."

In Byron's Don Juan occurs this musical verse:—

" 'Tis sweet to hear the watch-dog's honest bark,
   Bay deep mouthed welcome as we draw near home,
'Tis sweet to know there is an eye will mark
   Our coming and look brighter when we come."

Dear friends, you have come, you knew full well that we should welcome you *home* once more.

What does it signify? this coming into our midst, this jubilee day bedecked with sunshine and flowers, resonant in praises and bathed with prayer? Does it mean a kindly reception, a renewal of old acquaintance not forgot, a revival of the tender and sacred memories of childhood? Is it that you may revisit the rosy paths that lead to the hills or wander by the swiftly flowing Contoocook once again, or that you may with uncovered head read the names inscribed upon marble and stone, the names of those who once shared your joys and walked with you hand in hand to the sanctuary of the Lord God, learned the same lessons, acted well their part and have entered into their rest? Yes, and more—this, do not let us forget it is an anniversary of the "Church of Christ."

"Everything in Jesus Christ astonishes me," said the exiled Emperor of St. Helena—"the birth of Jesus, the story of his life, the profoundness of his doctrine which overturn all difficulties, his empire, his progress through all centuries is to me a prodigy." John Stewart Mills penned the following: "But as Jesus spake for eternity his truths ride on the wings of time; as he spoke for man they are welcome, beautiful and blessing wherever man is found and so must be till time and man shall cease." The coming of Christ, his career and abiding presence with his disciples, has made a profound impression upon the world! The record of the church is no mean one. The church of Christ need not be ashamed to hold a memorial over victories achieved under Christ, the Great Head of the church.

Without Christ in whose name this anniversary is called what better are we than Greece and Rome under Socrates and Cicero? I quote from Dr. Eliot: "Jesus Christ can do without us but we cannot do without him." Very true, without him right would have no sanction, and wrong no terror, and a pure life no lofty aspiration. My fellow mortals, the world is getting back to Christ, back to Christianity! If we take a wide survey, we note that:

> "Thro' the ages one unceasing purpose runs,
> And the hearts of men are
> Bettered with the process of the Suns."

The direction is plain, Emerson in his last years went back to the regular services of the denomination he thought he had outgrown. An able exponent of the Herbert Spencer philosophy at a dinner given in New York made two assertions, one as follows: "The proposition that men ought to do certain things and ought to refrain from doing certain things, and the *reason* why some things are wrong to do and others are right to do is in some mysterious but very real way connected with the existence and nature of this *divine power* which reveals itself in every great and every tiny thing, without which not a star courses in its nightly orbit and not a sparrow falls to the ground." My dear friends, this "Divine Power," recognized by the philosophy of the age, began 115 years ago, plus the Christian centuries of the past, it began to assert its power by "signs and wonders ;" it began with Jesus of Nazareth at the world's metropolis, where the great men were given to vices so debasing that to mention them would be to soil the paper from which I read, moreover benevolence was unknown, the poor and the orphan received neither justice nor mercy. There was not, in all pagandom, hospital, asylum or almshouse ; the face of things is changed. How so? The people, calling themselves Christians, banded together under covenant vows (vows made by Jehovah to the patriarchs and continued under Christ), have accomplished a great work! This work begins with the individual, it reaches out into and revolutionizes society. The church of Christ holds vice in check, raises the standard of morality to a maximum, teaches the soundest business principles, builds schools and colleges, multiplies Sabbath-schools, sends the Bible, the tract and the missionary of the Cross to the "remotest bounds of earth.' The trend of the Christian church is upward toward the skies! Her step is majestic like the sun and her purpose a holy one! Celebrate! Yes, friends, it is our right and duty so to do. The angels in choral symphony mark the triumphs of the cross, why not those rejoice who are made but a "little lower than the angles." This word, welcome, must now end. No festival of earth can afford more than a dim and distant picture of another gathering grander than *terrestrial jubilees!* When the soul, saved by the precious blood of Christ, shall stand in the glorified presence of Him to whom we offer our anthems to-day! We meet, welcome and part. Of this we are sure the sons and daughters of the Lord God will at last meet "around one common mercy seat." To use another's language, "Let the expectation of this be the inspiration of our life ; the fulfillment of that trust, let it be the glory of our immortality. Let every one be so alive in God's service in the earth that we may join in the worship of that immortal city, and forever, and forever more, our words shall be but the words of Him who spake in the Hebrew tongue," This is the Lord's doing ; it is marvellous in our eyes."

THE LORD IS ROUND HIS OWN.

I stood by the Holy City,
    Without the Damascus Gate,
While the wind blew soft from the distant sea,
    And the day was wearing late;
And swept its wide horizon
    With reverent lingering gaze,
From the rolling uplands of the west
    That slope a hundred ways,
To Olivet's gray terraces
    By Kedron's bed that rise,
Upon whose crest the crucified
    Was lost to mortal eyes;
And, far beyond, to the tawny line,
    Where the sun seemed still to fall,—
So bright the hue against the blue,
    Of Moab's mountain wall,
And north to the hills of Benjamin,
    Whose springs are flowing yet,
Ramah, and sacred Mizpah,—
    It's dome above them set;
And the beautiful words of the Psalmist
    Had meaning before unknown—
As the mountains are round Jerusalem
    The Lord is round his own.

In the fair Contoocook valley,
    Is a village as near to God
As the holy city of Palestine
    By saint and pilgrim trod;
A village with hills encircled,
    And waters as pure and cool
As those by the angel troubled
    In deep Siloam's pool;—
Crany hill on the south; and west
    The heights to Monadnock's marge;
And north the hills of Warner
    And the peak of lone Kearsarge;
I can see them still in the summer light,
    Now near, now faint and far,—
Their brows withdrawn as they had gone
    To mate with the morning star!
And I wonder yet if the lilies blow
    In the pond on Crany hill?
And the whispering pines above the stream
    Tower in their beauty still?

And along the shore if the river pinks
    Give spice to the air of June?
And the army brook through the meadow runs
    With its old melodious tune?
And the robin sings, and the bobolink,
    In the orchard trees and the clover?
And the brier-rose and sweet fern wave
    By the rocks, the pasture over?
Oh, I would give the bloom and balm
    Of every clime I know,
For the breath of the rose, and the fragrant fern
    Upon those slopes that grow!

And in this pleasant valley,
    Up from the river stands,
The Church whose founders long have dwelt
    Within the heavenly lands;
Whose aisles have seen a hundred years,
    The children come and go,
Till those who have passed to the upper realm
    Thrice number those below.
The bell may ring on Sabbath morns,
    But they will seek no more
By the winding roads adown the hills
    Its dear familiar door.
Pastors and people, one by one,
    Went home to their reward,
Their graves are in the church-yard nigh,
    Their souls are with the Lord;
But still their fervent prayers we hear
    From pulpit and from pew,
And still their hymns ring high and clear,
    Though they are lost to view!
Their memory to-day we bless;
    And, looking fondly back,
Pray that the church so dear to them
    God's presence may not lack;
But evermore its worshipers
    In life and death may prove
His gracious care, his faithfullness,
    His tender pitying love;
And say with the Hebrew psalmist,
    Where Zion's Temple shone,
As the mountains are round the valley
    The Lord is round his own!

                EDNA DEAN PROCTOR.

June, 1884.

THE CHURCH AS AN EDUCATOR.

BY HON. J. W. PATTERSON.

The history of education is indissolubly interwoven with that of the church. The possibility of mental development logically involves both the right and the duty of such development, but neither is realized by the unschooled.

The responsibilities, which the scriptures lay upon each human soul, awaken and enforce the obligation, and hence the priestly orders have been the ministers and promoters of education in every age.

In the earlier periods of civil society, the entire intellectual development of the people had its source and conduct in the ministers of religion, who founded institutions and monopolized the entire compass of human knowledge. The functionaries of the church mastered the limited circle of the sciences and professions, and became the astronomers, doctors, lawyers and statesmen of their day.

But the genius of Christianity is diffusive. Its dogmas are of universal application, and cannot be limited to a caste. Growth in knowledge and grace, which it inculcates, necessitates meditation upon the profoundest spiritual truths brought to our contemplation by revelation, and this involves that mental action which is the condition of growth. Inspiration styled the founder of Christianity a teacher and his followers disciples. The designation was literal, and hence teaching became a characteristic and historic function of the organized converts to the divine master. Intelligence is essential to spiritual life and the church advances with the intellectual progress of the race.

The Christians of the first centuries being unable to maintain schools of their own, educated their children at home or in the pagan schools. This was unfortunate for the simplicity and purity of their faith, and in 181 a school of the catechists was established by Pantaenus, in which the Christian faith was taught. Similar schools were also opened at Cæsarea, Antioch, Edessa and in other cities, where the Christians were in sufficient numbers to maintain them. But these schools were limited in number, and reached only a few of the children. In the fifth century, learning was driven into monasteries, where the monks, in their cells, studied and copied the priceless manuscripts of a classic age, and conserved the forces which in a better day were destined to regenerate the intellectual life of the world. In the sixth and seventh centuries, we find parochial, monastic and cathedral schools scattered through Italy, and a century later, the emperor Charlemagne founded similar seminaries of learning for the education of the people throughout his extended dominions. "Let us open schools," said the good monarch, "to teach the children to read; let in every monastery, in every bishopric, some one teach psalms, writing, arithmetic, grammar and employ correct copies of holy books; for often men seeking to pray to God, pray badly on account of the unfaithfulness of copyists."

At this time, all the great councils of the church were active in the same direction. "Let the priests in villages and towns hold schools," said the synod of Orleans, "in order that all the children entrusted to them can receive the first notion of letters." The council of Chalons decreed that bishops should establish schools where both literature and scripture should be taught.

This is in harmony with the decrees of other councils at that period. The educational system of Europe may be said to have been at that time in the direction of the church.

In an advanced and complex civilization, in which the social and civil status has been thoroughly defined and established, schools have been founded under the auspices of the state, or other than eclesiastical organizations, but even then they have required the countenance and patronage of the religious orders. This is true in pagan as in Christian communities. In India and Egypt in which ancient philosophy and learning found their earliest and highest development, the schools were directed and moulded exclusively by the priestly castes. The religious order of the Magi, who were the highest officers and dignitaries of state at the courts of Media and Persia, had the full control of the intellectual culture of those ancient empires. Under the theocratic institutions of the Hebrews, the schools of the prophets, and, after the return from the captivity, the schools of the synagogue, in which the national history and traditions, the writings of inspired prophets and poets and the biblical ethics and philosophy were discussed and recited, were founded by religious teachers and conducted under their auspices. They were rather associations of scholars than schools, in which the wise men sat upon a raised platform and the younger disciples upon the floor, like Paul at the feet of Gamaliel. It was in one of these schools that our Savior was found by his parents discussing with the elders the great questions of the law.

The schools of Greece, in which pure intellectual power reached its culmination and did its most imperishable work, seem to have been secular and political rather than sacerdotal. But it should be borne in mind, that the Greek scholar lit his torch at an Egyptian altar which was kept aflame by the priestly orders.

The intellectual life of Rome was a simple development of the Greek system under new conditions and by a coarser and more masculine race.

The political convulsions which followed the death of the great emperor, left only the Episcopal and conventual schools as the fruit of his labors. Following hard upon the reign of Charlemagne, Alfred the Great of England invited to his court men of the highest intellectual eminence, established schools in all parts of his kingdom, and "ordained that the children of *every free man whose circumstances would allow it*, should acquire the arts of reading and writing, and that those designed for civil or ecclesiastical office, should be instructed in the Latin language." If Alfred did not found the University of Oxford, he certainly gave substantial aid to the monastic schools established where it now is. But the night of the tenth century settled upon Europe and the light of learning only lingered in the cloisters. The schools retreated to these seclusions of the church and awaited the renaissance. Driven in upon themselves, the monks turned to a close and critical study of the old manuscripts upon their dusty shelves, and the spirit of a higher and stronger intellectual life began to stir within those sleeply cells and impel to action. The result was the founding, during the twelfth century, of the great universities in which students passed beyond the trivium and quadrivium into the profounder philosophy and literature of the classic ages. But all of these institutions except the Italian, like those of Bologna and Salerno, which were in their origin professional schools, originated in the monastic and cathedral schools. It is said that up to the thirteenth century not half a dozen lay teachers were employed in all these universities. The renaissance had its roots in the institutions of the church, and the influence of the church may be traced in its marvelous results.

It is impossible to calculate the power which has been exerted by the great universities in moulding the destinies of Europe. But they did not reach the wants of the laboring poor. The institutions erected by Charlemagne in all parts of his vast dominions, would have done so, had not his noble purpose been defeated by the anarchy which followed his death. To the mass of the people groveling in slavery, degradation and misery at the base of society, the cloistral schools brought no light and gave no hope.

At the very midnight of popular ignorance in Europe, science was winning new trophies and erecting her temples within all lands reached by the jurisdiction of Arabia. But the uplifting of the working substratum of society in the west, only came with the reformation. It was this great religious awakening, which gave birth to institutions for the intellectual and moral elevation of the masses of mankind.

In 1528 Luther and Melanchthon prepared a curriculum of studies for the common schools, which, by their influence, were being organized through Germany. Zwingle, Calvin, and all the great reformers which followed, laboring in the spirit of their master, supplemented the measures which had been inaugurated by the imperial intellect of Luther, for the education of the people. In this way it came about, that the German schools which sprung from the Reformation, became the germ and pattern of the system which spread over a large part of Europe, and prevailed for three centuries.

Thus, as we see, it was the spirit and power of the church which conceived and consummated this phenomenal work, than which there had been nothing more promotive of human welfare in the records of any Christian state.

But even the schools, which sprang from the Reformation, did not open the portals of knowledge to all. The honor of founding a system of public instruction free to every child, and maintained at the expense of the state, was reserved to the Puritans of New England, who, in the fatherland, had imbibed the political ethics of the Reformation. Here no hereditary privileges or class monopolies prevented the realization of that equality of rights which was the genius of their Christian creed. There was a logical and historic connection between the Reformation and the establishment of free institutions on these shores. The equality of souls before the law of God, which is a Scriptural tenet of the church, has inspired every movement for the development and freedom of the human mind.

Cotton Mather assigned the low estate of the schools of learning in the old country as one of the reasons for the emigration of the Puritans, and in a very brief period after settlement. our pious ancestors established schools in all the New England colonies, corresponding to those which had been destroyed by the thirty years' war in Germany.

These were not strictly free schools, but in 1643 both Massachusetts and Connecticut took action looking to the establishment of common schools to be supported by a general tax. It was not till 1647, however, that an act was passed by the old Bay Colony, which, for the first time in the history of the world, gave to all the children of a state a system of free public schools. This was the first and the type of our American system of common schools; and, if any man doubts the influence of the church in this imperishable act of statesmanship, let him read the following preamble to the law :

" It being one chiefe project of that old deluder. Satan. to keep men from the knowledge of the Scriptures, as in former times, keeping them in an unknowne tongue, so in these latter times, by perswading them from the use of tongues, so that at least the true sence and meaning of the originall might bee clouded with false glosses of saint seeming deceivers ; and that learning may not bee buried in the grave of our forefathers in church and commonwealth, the Lord assisting our indeavors : *It is therefore ordered by this courte and authority thereof,"* etc.

From that day until this the churches of America, and preeminently the ministers of religion, have given their influence and support to the schools of learning in all their grades. As these two institutions were laid by the fathers as a sub-structure to the state, so they stand to-day a mutual support, giving unity and durability to the republic.

In the absence of definite records, it is impossible to resolve the educational work of any locality, and assign to each agency the proportionate share of influence which it has given to the process. It would be as easy to analyze a harvest and assign to the earth, the rain, and the sunshine, the force and the elements which each had contributed to the general result. So I am baffled in any attempt to designate, with precision, the part which the dear old church, of which I became a member at the age of fifteen, played in the educational affairs of Henniker. But for a hundred and fifteen years we can trace its influence, woven like golden threads into the fabric which stretches through four generations of our townsmen. Take from the web this spiritual tracery, and our work would have been as unavailing as the weaving of Penelope.

The church was organized in 1769, the year of the founding of Dartmouth College. Two years earlier, there had been a private school in town, and four years later, my great-grandmother, Elizabeth Arbuckle Patterson, who was a native of the Atlantic ocean, as she was born during the voyage of her parents from the north of Ireland, taught a public school, and was paid out of the first money raised for that purpose. Whether the church exerted any direct influence in establishing a system of public instruction in the town or not, we cannot say, but we learn from the town history, that Rev. Moses Sawyer was chairman of the first school committee, and that the ministers and leading members of the church have been prominent in the educational records of the town down to the present time.

This is very observable in tracing the fluctuating but honorable history of the "old academy." While we find among its founders, officers and patrons, the names of excellent and efficient citizens, not members of the church, yet the majority of its earliest and most active friends have been prominent in promoting the religious welfare of the community. Some of these have contributed liberally to the education of poor students, who, from time to time, have struggled through this institution, and gone forth to the activities and honors of the world.

I deem it a special felicity that I cannot recall one of all who have here laid the foundations of their intellectual life, who has dishonored the institution or the place of his nativity. Col. Cogswell has given us the names of twenty-four college graduates of Henniker, but this list is only a fragment of the long roll of the sons and daughters of the town who have fitted in its schools for an honorable part in the drama of life. Many have passed from the stage, but we linger to rehearse the past. The way is long and thick with graves, but to-day we will unsphere the garnered years and repeople the haunts of our childhood with the living and the dead to "memory dear." Brilliant achievements and splendid successes have marked the decades as they have passed, but sad failures and bitter disappointments have mingled with the triumphs and dispelled the illusions of youth. The retrospects of life temper with doubts the prophecies of the young. Something of the repose and sadness of autumn succeeds to the spring-tide vigor and assurance of our school days. Never again shall we see boys quite so brave and handsome and full of promise, or bright-eyed girls, quite so fair and spirited and full of grace, as the school-mates of our youth. These were the peerless beings of our golden age, which has passed. But the real life of these idealized friends of early years was grander and nobler than the dream-life, which our fancies foreshadowed for them. Many trod the path of toil and sorrow, but their souls grew strong, and they were spiritual victors in the issue of the struggle. One ascended on a strong, melodious wing into the realm of song, and another thundered at the gates of oppression; some fought for liberty in the arbitrament of blood, and others plead for the right in the assemblies of the people; some bore the torch of revelation into the night of paganism, and others guided the mental powers into the domain of knowledge; some accepted the responsibilities and bore the hardships of public life, and others pushed into the arena of business, or developed their paternal estates. But all, in whatever field of enterprise or labor they moved, bore themselves with a disciplined intelligence, a courageous temper, and an honest purpose. It has been my fortune to listen to the famous orators of the age in this and other lands, and I do not recall one, who surpassed in the gift of native eloquence the cherished friend of my boyhood, whom some of you well remember in the debates of our village club. Beloved and honored of all, he was cut down by a mysterious Providence in the promise of early manhood. Others with parts, it may be less rare but not less useful, went forth from our schools, inspired and sustained by the truths which successive generations have been taught in this house of God, and have made an imperishable impress upon the industries, institutions and peoples, among whom their lots have been cast. Christian schools are the well-springs of our Christian civilization, and that has transformed the world. The schools awaken inventive genius that indefinitely multiplies the productive power of labor, quickens the enterprise that is the parent of comprehensive schemes of business, and creates aspirations for lofty achievements and a noble life. The schools and the churches of New England, working together, have made her sons the conservators of states, and her daughters the mothers of a noble race. The venerable church, planted in this place thirty years before the close of the last century, had a stormy history for a generation, but since its separation from the state has been signally fortunate in the men chosen to minister at its altar. Of the living, known to you all, I need not speak. The Rev. Moses Sawyer tradition represents as a man of strong character, and great dignity of manner. His successor, the Rev. Jacob Scales, was the minister of my childhood whom I recall with great reverence and respect. He was a man of learning, and possessed a keen, incisive intellect, that was deceived by no sophistry, and struck at sham and pretense with a sarcasm as sharp as Ithuriel's spear. But he interested himself in all the affairs of the town and abetted every good cause. The spiritual and intellectual welfare of the young were very near his heart, and he co-operated earnestly with other public-spirited citizens, in establishing the Henniker Academy, for which I, and many others, now widely scattered, shall never cease to be grateful.

He was followed be the Rev. Eden Foster, who possessed an intellect as rich and fertile in its orginal powers of thought and expression, as Edmund Burke's, and was gifted with a nature as sensitive and affectionate as a woman's. No person ever knew Eden Foster but to love him, and no person ever felt his influence who was not made better. The spirit that emenated from these ministers of religion, inspired the church and prevaded the whole community. In the schools it was an assimilating and organizing force, building into a consistent unity of character all acquisitions of knowledge and personal experience, and so elevating the tone and intelligence of the general public.

The immediate agency of the church as an educator has been positive and absolute through all the Christian centuries, and is still active in conventual, parochial and denominational schools, but the invisible influence of religious truth, permeating the whole mass of society like some hidden force of nature, has been the paramount power through which the church has moulded and revolutionized the intellectual and moral activities of the world.

All great movements spring from some germinal force acting from the center outward. Such forces are discoverable everywhere in nature from the stellar systems to the crystals upon your window pane. Social organisms, business enterprises, governments and civilizations are evolutions of esoteric energies. So the founder of our faith, in conformity to the established order, made love the central power of his kingdom. The apostle was commanded to sheathe his sword, for love was the fulfilling of the law in the new dispensation. This to the spiritual is what gravitation is to the natural world, an organizing and controlling power, slowly eliminating perturbations and developing its absolute control over human history. The church is the visible representative of this spiritual kingdom, and is only legitimate in its workings, when its methods are dictated and inspired by love. Christ was sometimes stern and severe in the utterance and defense of truth as his followers must be, but the controlling spirit through all is love.

In the grand march of the church through human events, like its divine founder, it has brought light and uplifting to the mind as to the heart of the race. Sometimes seduced by the love of power, it has placed fetters upon the human intellect, but whenever and wherever it has moved in the spirit of its master, it has founded schools and universities, and devoted its re-sources and its power to the diffusion of knowledge. The foundation of arbitrary power resting upon the ignorance of the masses has crumbled; the reign of slavery is over, and barbarism is being driven from the uttermost parts of the earth by the spread of intelligence. Ingenuity, quickened in the schools, is lifting the race from the bondage of toil and leading it up to truer and grander views of the economy of grace. These are of the triumphs of the church moving in the spirit of love through the schools which it has founded.

MUSIC, CHOIRS AND CHORISTERS.

BY HON. OLIVER PILLSBURY.

In the absence of a single line of records the task assigned me is, to say the least, somewhat embarrassing. Memory is unreliable in the classification of details even for the period it covers. Tradition omits, mixes and exaggerates, frequently affording only a mass of irreconcilable incongruities to be culled and arranged by presumptive probabilities. The result is then liable to partake of the prejudices as well as the judgment of the person using them. Strict chronological accuracy is out of the question. I trust you will therefore moderate your expectations and be merciful in your criticisms.

You will allow me, when I have occasion to refer to individuals, to use the names they were familiarly known by when the events occurred.

It may safely be taken for granted that the early usages adopted in this town did not differ materially from those prevailing in religious assemblies generally in New England down to the present century. Tate and Brady's collection of hymns, at first used, were early superseded by Dr. Watts' Psalms and Hymns which became the standard, and congregational singing was the universal custom. "Worcester's Collection" and "The Village Harmony" furnished the tunes for a long period. It was customary to choose a leader to "set the tune" or "tune the psalm" as it was called. He was prominently located in front of the congregation near the deacon's seat and usually a few of the best singers were seated near by as supports. The hymn or psalm having been announced, and sometimes read, he named the tune, gave the pitch upon a wooden instrument called a "pitch pipe" and then read two lines, usually, which the congregation were expected to join with him in singing ; then two lines more were read and sung, and so on to the end of the hymn. This was called *lining* and some times *deaconing* the hymn, probably from the fact that one of the deacons was generally the leader, or precentor, as they were called, if capable of filling the position. It required very close attention on the part of the leader as well as the congregation to retain the pitch of the tune and remember the words to be sung*. The tunes were ordinarily strong and lively. Fugues, in which the parts slid or tumbled in one after another and closed with a stirring chorus that made the very walls of the church tremble were very popular. The minor tunes, now seldom heard at all, were indispensable on funeral and other solemn occasions. The high cost and scarcity of books was relieved by this method and it also had the merit of placing all upon an equality, and inviting and enabling all to join in the devotional exercises. Samuel Mansfield was chosen at different times by this town to "tune the psalm" prior to the beginning of the present century and there is evidence extant that Amos Gould performed this duty still later. This custom probably prevailed in this town until the settlement of Rev. Moses Sawyer in 1802 and possibly a little later. There is no mention either in history or tradition of an organized choir prior to this time. It must be borne in mind that until about the time Mr. Sawyer was settled the church and State were united and every movement of importance was voted by the town. The settlement of Mr. Sawyer virtually achieved the separation of church and State in this town, inasmuch as he was settled by the "Calvinistic Congregational Society" acting independently of the town, although the "toleration act" was not passed by the legislature until 1819.

At the new era then commenced it is probable that a choir was organized. Tradition says that both Mr. Sawyer and his

---

*Mr. Pillsbury here gave a brief verbal account of his experience forty-nine years ago as precentor of a large congregation in New Jersey where he was engaged in teaching, and particularly of a County Sabbath-school anniversary occasion at which Hon. Theodore Frelinghuysen, then Chancellor of New York University, was the orator of the day. The hymns were *lined* and sung by the vast assemblage with great power.

wife were very good singers and that a choir was early organized at their solicitation under the leadership of "Master John Connor." Mr. Connor, who occupied a large space in the history of music in this town for more than half a century, was then about 24 years old. He was teaching singing schools all about and had already acquired great fame as a singer and musician. He possessed a rich musical voice of great range and compass of which he had perfect command, throwing it from one part to another where most needed or where he could be most effective. He had a way frequently, especially when singing the last tune, of pouring out an excelsior strain an octave above the key of such sweetness and power as to startle the whole congregation; and some of them used to say the sound rung in their ears all the week.

He was supported at this period by his brothers, George and Abel, Solomon and Josiah Childs, the Morrisons, Howes, Campbells and Pattersons, and a little later by Dyer Abbott and James Atkinson, and still later by the Goulds and Fosters all of whom were more or less musical families.

Mr. Connor claimed the credit, and no doubt justly, of developing the vocal powers of several girls, as he used to call them, and particularly of Lucinda Gould, whose memory will long be cherished by this people for her many virtues and great force of character. She was doubtless the most attractive and accomplished lady singer who has ever resided in the town. Bass viols, violins and some wind instruments had already come into use. Mr. Connor was very skillful with the former and doubtless did much to further the cultivation of instrumental as well as vocal music.

We are not informed that anything occurred out of the ordinary course, or worthy of special mention, for quite a number of years. Mr. Connor and Mr. Abbott both taught singing schools occasionally, but do not appear ever to have become alienated from each other, Mr. Connor retained the position of chorister and Mr. Abbott sustained him. Matters went on in this way until the winter of 1823 and '24. Mr. Connor, as might have been expected, had grown somewhat imperious and was naturally very outspoken and sharp in his reproofs and criticisms.

This created friction and a strong movement sprung up for a change. Liberal subscriptions were obtained and the services of Dea. Ezra Barrett of Warner, a very popular teacher of music, were secured for the winter. This school was conducted afternoon and evening in Bartlett's Hall, which was in the house now occupied by George W. Rice. The hall was arranged with two rows of seats on three sides with tables in the center for the instrumental performers. The "Bridgewater Collection" of tunes was used. The attendance was very large, embracing many new beginners and nearly all the musical talent in the town. The school was a great success and closed with a grand public concert in the church. Dea. Barrett also taught the next winter with unabated success.

Large accessions were made to the choir from these schools, Mr. Connor still retaining the choristership. The choir extended each way from the center of the gallery opposite the pulpit of the church, that was burned, to and around the corners occupying two rows of seats. Instead of massing all the best singers at the center a prominent one or two was stationed at the extremes to hold up and sustain the weak and faltering. Mr. Abbott's post for years was at the extreme right. Among the new family names added to the choir at this time were Woods, Rice, Whitney, Pillsbury, Gibson, Searles, Cogswell, Smith, Livingstone and doubtless others besides recruits from families already named. The choir was doubtless more numerous at this time than at any other period. Of bass viol players of the town, in addition to the Connors, may be mentioned Col. Imri Woods, Dr. Sanborn, Samuel Morrison, William and Jeremiah Foster, Carlos Gould, and later Hiram Rice, Luther Whitcomb and Washington Cogswell. William Foster, at the solicitation of the choir, made a double bass viol for their use, saying at the outset that he could make something and if it didn't work he could use it for a grain chest. This viol was burned with the meeting-house. The principal violinists were Col. Woods, Perley and Micah Howe, Worcester Goss, and later the younger Howes and the far famed Columbus Gibson. Of the clarionet players, a very popular instrument fifty years ago, may be named Carlos Gould, who also played the flute, Frederick Whitney, J. W. Pillsbury, Frederick and Dutton Woods, Goodale Childs, Daniel C. Gould, and Uri Smith. Robert Eaton later played the flute. Nearly all of this list of musicians at one time or another rendered assistance in the singing schools and in the choir.

Matters appear to have moved on successfully from the date of the Barrett schools without much change other than members occasionally dropping out until the winter of 1831 and '32. In the mean time, however, Col. Woods had become chorister, but at what date cannot now be determined. A strong movement was now made for another school, to include beginners, which proved successful. This was also held in Bartlett's hall and was taught by Col. Woods. It introduced new family names—Colby, Whitcomb, Bartlett and doubtless others, but was mainly recruited from those already named. The families of those days were famous for furnishing recruits, numbering, as they did, from half a score to a full baker's dozen, they held out from twenty to twenty-five years as recruiting stations. This school was also very satisfactory and served to replenish the choir. Both were strongly supported by instrumental performers.

The next event of interest to the choir was the dedication of this church, which occurred in 1834. In anticipation of this event the musical talent of the town was assembled and it was voted to procure the "National Choir," which contained particularly appropriate selections for dedicatory occasions. This necessitated meetings for practice which were fully attended by singers and instrumental performers, all under the direction of Col. Woods, whose proverbially winning and conciliatory ways harmonized the different elements and thus secured musical harmony which contributed much to make the occasion pleasing and satisfactory.

About this time choirs were organized for the two other churches erected that same year. This divided the musical talent of the town and full union schools were at an end ; although no unpleasantness worthy of remark ever appeared.

The next year the first church organ was procured. This displaced some instrumental performers who had been strong supporters of the choir and since there was no one in town then who could play the organ, it was thought by some at least, Mr. Connor and Col. Woods among them, that a great mistake had been made. Dr. Sanborn took charge of the organ but could not devote sufficient time to it to become an acceptable player, consequently there were long intervals in which it was scarcely opened. Bass viols, violins and other instruments were invited back into the choir again.

At length, however, the services of Maria Woods, who was then giving much attention to musical study, were secured to take charge of the organ. After her followed, in turn, Miss Chaffin and Miss Mills, who were employed here as music teachers in a select school. Then the late Washington Cogswell became the organist and continued such many years. It is worthy of remark that he was doubtless connected with the choir more consecutive years than any other person who was ever a member. He was succeeded as organist by his sister, Susan, who continued as such until she removed to Minnesota. She was followed by Susan Webster, who occupied the position quite a number of years. Mrs. Warren Clark succeeded her and was the organist until she removed to Concord in 1870. Shortly after this Carrie Morse became the organist and has continued as such until the present time. Others have played the organ, more or less, to fill up gaps or in the absence of the regular organist. Among them we recall Henrietta Wilkins, Mary Childs, Lucy Chandler, Mrs. Julia Folsom, Enoch Colby, Minnie Cogswell and Mrs. Hoffman.

The organ now in use was procured in 1871 largely through the liberality of Dea. Horace Childs and Mr. A. D. L. F. Connor.

In 1836 another very popular singing school was conducted in the academy by Mr. Breed Batchelder, who was the first professor employed in that institution. This school was very fully attended, bringing in the family names of Wallace, Wilkins, Campbell, Barnes, Peters and doubtless others, with many new recruits from families already named. A very satisfactory public concert was given in the church at its close. This school also served to replenish the choir. Daniel C. Gould was chosen chorister at this time and retained the position until he left town, probably in 1842.

Singing schools, other than those I have noted, have been frequent, taught by residents and others, all the way along down to the present time for the benefit of the choir; but have not been so numerously attended, if we except Prof. Ben. Davis' schools which embraced all ages and classes without much reference to any choir.

Among the teachers, not already named, may be mentioned Leonard Marshall, of Boston; Mr. Cheney, of Holderness; Frederick Whitney, Mr. Gay, of Francestown; Mr. Atwood, Mr. Chandler, of Antrim; Imri S. Whitney, Mr. Barton, of Newport; Mr. Ingalls, of Concord; Benjamin Colby, Worcester Morrison, Harris W. Campbell and Enoch Colby. Julia A. Childs, Maria Woods and Mrs. Warren Clark, all of whom stood at the head of the choir, more or less, taught juvenile classes for the benefit of the Sabbath-school, and several very interesting public exhibitions were given.

Nearly all these schools, except the juvenile classes, have been supported by voluntary contributions and were thus made free to all. This speaks well for the liberality of the town and society. As the result of this liberality and public spirit the musical talent has been developed and the town has always been favored with an unusual share of acceptable performers. It would be pleasant to call attention to many individual names, but lack of time will not permit. Without doubt the native musical genius of John Connor, starting away back in the last century, had much to do with giving tone and shaping the drift of musical culture and progress in the town. He was endowed with exquisite musical taste and often used to say "Noise is not music." A few months before his death, at the age of 83, he selected the hymns, tunes and singers for his funeral; and the last direction given to a friend only a few hours before his death was "sing softly." Col. Woods also did much for the cultivation of music, as also did Frederick Whitney by his long and unabated interest. He was chorister at different times, assisted latterly by his estimable wife. Of non-residents, descendants of the town, may be named Imri S. Whitney, who made musical science his life work, having taught successfully many years in Manchester and elsewhere, Seth Abbott, son of Dyer Abbott, already named, has achieved notority as a singer, and his daughter, Emma Abbott, has charmed both hemispheres with her peerless vocal performances. She is now at the head of a noted opera troupe. Your own inimitable Gibson has carried the artistic musical standard so high that it is scarcely probable the town will again reach it in another century.

Notwithstanding the fact that all the schools may have brought recruits to the choir, the membership has been diminishing for many years, owing, in part, to the scarcity of young people and in part, it is believed, to lack of interest or desire to become singers ; other amusements being more attractive, for the time being, but, as we believe, far less satisfactory in the long run. This, we regret to say, is the case otherwheres. In the cities, where there is no lack for numbers, expensive quartette choirs is the rule. They are simply quasi theatrical performers who please and entertain, while the real worshippers are left to take up the refrain (in silence of course). "Hosannas languish on our tongues, and our devotion dies."

To say the current has alway run evenly, without jars, jealousies or rivalries, would doubtless be saying too much, since the members of the choir have been human. It is gratifying, however, to be able to say, that it is believed these temporary discords have left no lasting alienations of friendship. They have generally resulted from the indiscreet remarks and meddlesome criticisms of outsiders whose preferences and judgment were allowed to have undue weight. The choir has been sustained all these many years by volunteers and performed its part in the devotional exercises acceptably to the congregation and we trust acceptably to Him who has endowed us with powers to make melody in our hearts and sing His praise.

Of those who have been choristers not already named may be mentioned, Asa Whitney, Benjamin Colby, Imri S. Whitney, Worcester Morrison, Ephraim Goss, Enoch Colby and Harris

W. Campbell, who is the present chorister, supported on the right by Mrs. Sarah Goss.*

The present choir† is here to speak for itself and needs no commendation from me. It is sad to reflect that time will make inroads upon it as has been the case in the past. We trust, however, that the long procession of its members, who have crossed to the other shore, are chanting in nobler strains than they were permitted to utter here. It is devoutly hoped that, as one after another falls by the way, others will stand ready to take up the songs of the sanctuary; that as the Lord God promised the Hebrew King that he should not want a man to stand before Him forever, so there may never be wanting a choir to stand before Him and this people in this beautiful earthly Temple.

*Societies have been formed, from time to time, for practice and mutual improvement. In the winter of 1879 the choir extended invitations to all persons who had ever been members to meet them in reunion. Quite a large number responded in person and others by letter. The occasion was very enjoyable.

†Names of present members of the choir:—*Tenor*, Harris W. Campbell, leader, E. P. Goss; *Bass*, H. A. Emerson, R. L. Childs, O. A. Newton; *Soprano*, Mrs. E. P. Goss, Mrs. Josiah Emery, Sarah M. Peabody, Anna J. Newton, Minnie A. Cogswell; *Alto*, Mrs. Horace Childs, Mrs Geo. C. Preston, Mrs. H. W. Campbell, Mrs. Washington Cogswell; *Organist*, Carrie L. Morse.

ANNIVERSARY HYMN.—NO. 1

I.

More precious, Lord, than sands of gold,
    Or perfumes of the storied East,
Thy mercies from the days of old,
    Thy favors year by year increased!
To-day our hearts and hands we raise,
    Like climbing vines that seek the sun,
In glad and grateful songs of praise,
    For battles fought and triumphs won!

II.

As to the humble, saintly ones
    A hundred years ago and more,
In winter's frosts and summer's suns,
    The flying days Thy blessing bore;
So to the children's children now,
    Who tread the paths their feet have trod,
And at the self-same altar bow,
    Thy favor show, most gracious God.

III.

Make more and more Thy grace abound;
    Give to Thy saving word success;
Through saintly lives Thy gospel sound
    Abroad, and needy nations bless!
Here let a faithful people give
    Thee homage to the latest time,
In faith, and love, and union live,
    And ripen for a Heavenly Clime!

ANNIVERSARY HYMN.—NO. 2.

Tune, Portuguese Hymn.

I.

With gladness we come to Thy temple, O Lord,
    To tell of Thy goodness for many a day;
The covenant gifts of Thy grace to record,
    So signally crowning and blessing the way.

II.

The Church of Thy planting, well watered and fed,
    Well nourished and guarded and quickened by Thee,
Continues to flourish and graciously shed
    The light of Thy word o'er the land and the sea.

III.

Here fathers and mothers have labored and prayed,
    And sown the good seed with a liberal hand;
Have finished their work, and the summons obeyed
    With confident hope in Thy presence to stand!

IV.

Here children with filial devotion to-day,
    Are bearing the burdens they heartily bore,
Rejoicing with patience to labor and pray,
    Till places that know them shall know them no more.

V.

Thy blessing, our Father, we pray Thee bestow;
    Thy promise, remember, to be with Thine own!
Give wisdom the virtues and graces to grow,
    And garner in Heaven when the harvest is grown!

THE MISSION WORK OF THE CHURCH.

BY REV. WILLIAM WOOD.

ELIZABETH PROCTOR,

sister of Mrs. Judge Darling, and of Dea. John Proctor, was born in Ipswich, Mass., Feb. 1st, 1773. She professed religion in Hopkinton, N. H., Nov. 1810, studied at Rev. Joseph Emerson's school, Byfield, Mass. She was one of the four female teachers of the first four classes of small children gathered into our Sunday-school in 1815. In 1822 she went a missionary to the Cherokee Indians in Georgia. She pursued her journey alone through the wilderness, on foot and on horseback, fording rivers and enduring many hardships. She reached High Tower in the Cherokee nation Feb. 14, 1823. For four years she taught among the Indians. In 1827 she married Rev. Daniel Sabin Buttrick, a missionary of the A. B. C. F. M. in the same field, with whom she labored until her death August 3, 1847.

CASSANDER SAWYER,

daughter of Rev. Moses Sawyer, second pastor of this church, was born June 24, 1809. She professed religion at Chilicothe, Ohio, 1829; studied at Ipswich Female Seminary under Miss Grant and Miss Lynn. September 22, 1833, she married Rev. Jesse Lockwood. In October of the same year she left with her husband for Dwight Station, in the Cherokee nation, where they arrived Jan. 25, 1834. Her husband died in the July following; the next year she returned home to her father's house, where she remained till her death, June 23, 1840.

TIMOTHY DARLING,

son of Judge Darling, born Dec. 24, 1798, was one of the fourteen persons composing the first class for the study of the Bible in our Sunday-school, in 1814. He was a graduate of Harvard, studied law and practiced in Hillsboro' and Loudon, this state. in Richmond, Va., and Ypsilanti, Michigan. He afterwards studied theology at Gilmanton, and was under the Home Missionary Society from June 1, 1846, to June 1, 1850, and ministered to the Congregational Church of South Wales, N. Y.

REV. JOSIAH HILL

and his wife Abigail (Bacon) Hill united with this church Feb. 8, 1818. I remember them in my earlier years as residing in the house nearest the school-house in "Westbury Corner." About the year 1826 or '27 he entered upon a course of study for the ministry. He was ordained and preached at Lynnfield, Mass. While there he visited Henniker, preached for Rev. Mr. Scales and also one evening in the Westbury Corner schoolhouse. I have been able to gather very little of their career. It would seem that their work was of the nature of home missionary work, that on leaving Lynnfield they went west, which meant, in those days, the state of New York and Michigan, perhaps, where they were lost sight of.

MARY L. WADSWORTH,

daughter of Titus Vespartian and Susanna (Warde) Wardsworth, was born May 17, 1836. At the age of 15 she united with the church at Franklin. In 1861 she graduate at South Hadley Female Seminary. She entered the profession of a teacher, but afterward studied medicine, graduating first in her class in 1867 from the Female Medical College, Philadelphia. She practised her profession at Springfield. Excelling in the practice of medicine, she was in three years invited by her Alma Mater (South Hadley) to become teacher and practicing physician in that institution. At the same time she received a most urgent request from the Woman's Board of Foreign Missions to go to Constantinople to labor as a Missionary physician among the Mohammedans. She accepted this invitation, and in 1871 left home for that distant city. Not finding ready access to the Mohammedans, her practice was confined to mission families, and the Armenians and Bulgarians. This was no small field. Failing health led her to the cooler regions of Asia Minor; while there she became acquainted with Dr. John Bassian, of Brousa, a native of that country, but a graduate of Michigan University, and was united with him in marriage in 1873, since which time they have practiced medicine in that city.

SOCRATES SMITH,

son of Ezekiel and Abigail (Wilder) Smith, was born June 16, 1814. April 29, 1835, he united with this church, at the age of twenty-one. Like most young men of the town he grew up to hard work on the farm. The spirit of the age for better means to a higher education began about this time to take possession of the leading men of our town. He was in the Henniker Academy two years, and graduated at Dartmouth College in 1842. He entered Union Theological Seminary, N.Y. After three years he married Lydia Maria Harwood, and entered at once upon Home Mission work in the West, under the American Home Missionary Society. He served churches at Beardstown, Panther Creek, Jerseyville, and Troy, Ill., also taught at Greenville for three years. He died in 1869. In the Academy and in College and Theological Seminary, Mr. Smith was a hard working student. He had a hard struggle with poverty. I entered the seminary after he had been there two years, and he told me himself that he had lived for many a week on 12½ cents a week. A slice of dry bread dipped in a little poor molasses made his meal. Dr. Coe, Hon. Secretary of the American Home Missionary Society, in a letter to me, gives this testimony to him: "He had the confidence and esteem of the conductors of the society as a faithful and useful missionary."

ELIZABETH DARLING,

daughter of Joshua and Mary (Proctor) Darling, was born

Jan. 5, 1812, about a month before the first missionary band of the American Board—Hall, Nott, Rice, Judson and Newell—sailed for their mission field in the Eastern world. When a young girl Mrs. B. read a memoir of Harriet Newell, and after it was finished she said to her mother that she wanted to be like Harriet Newell and become a missionary. Her mother, laying her hand on her head, said, "My dear, I trust that when you are older you will engage in the same work." We cannot doubt that this little incident had much to do in giving shape to her whole life and character. I can, in the time allotted, give but a faint outline of her useful life. From the incident related it is evident that her heart was drawn to the service of the Lord from a child. She united with the church in 1832. In the meantime she was improving her mind at home and elsewhere with a view of teaching. Derry of this state and Ipswich of Massachusetts were, at this time, celebrated for their seminaries for young ladies. She studied at both and graduated at the latter taking high rank as a scholar. May 5, 1835, she married Rev. Henry Ballantine of Marion, Ohio. On the 16th of May they embarked from Boston in a sailing vessel for Bombay, and arrived there on the 11th of Oct., following. After one year at Bombay, devoted to the study of the Marathi language, they went to Ahmednagar, which city and state was the field for their life work. Not the first to enter this field, yet their work was largely pioneer work. Their home was in the heart of the city, a city of 30,000 people. Their house is a Mohammedan structure of massive stone walls six feet thick, with an upper story. It is flat roof overlooking the city. This is a favorite resort of the missionaries for a breath of pure, cool, evening air. The yard of their home contains about two acres. In this yard are Mrs. Ballantine's school-houses and others for native helpers and native Christians who clung close to the missionary in early days for support and protection. This was the scene of Mrs. B.'s labors for thirty years, with the exception of two or three years spent in America. During these years she had charge of "Christian Girls' School" spending from three or four hours daily in the school. Besides this she selected and took to her home some of the scholars and spent much time in teaching them the Bible. There are many well educated Christian women, graduates of this school who are now wives and mothers, guiding well their households, and are usefully employed not only in our missions but in the missions of other societies in Western India. As many mothers came to reside here and care for their children, Mrs. Ballantine would gather them at some hour, usually at noon, and Christian or heathen, daily, read and teach them the Holy Scriptures. Most of the girls of this school were brought into the church. The printed reports for eight years, 1857–'64, say that 39 girls were received to the church, an average of five yearly. At that time the school, for lack of accommodations, numbered but 50. Within a few years a nice, large schoolhouse has been built and the number of pupils is now 150. The zenana work in those days had not opened up so fully as now, as the door of access to them opened Mrs. Ballantine entered upon this work with great diligence and zeal. One would think that, with all these duties and cares, she had little to do with household affairs, not so, she had servants but everything was carefully superintended by herself. A plain, but well spread, table around which her large family gathered three time a day, with the regularity of South Hadley rules, was a picture of rare felicity and beauty. In a visit of the deputation to the missions of India in 1854, Dr. Anderson pronounced Mrs. Ballantine "a model housekeeper." The mental and religious training of her children depended largely upon her. There were no schools for them at Ahmednagar. With the rudiments of a good education from their parents the children all ranked high in the schools and colleges of this country where they came to finish their education. A life of such toil for thirty years is a great work and a great tax upon one's energies, but in such a climate as India it can be perform by few. Hard, incessant work at last broke down the health of Mr. Ballantine and in the autum of 1865 the parents, with their two children then with them, left India for America. Mr. Ballantine died off Portugal and was buried in the Atlantic ocean. For the last nine years Mrs. Ballantine has found a home at Amherst, Mass She could not return to India but her heart is there. Her elder daughter, Mary, married Mr. Fairbanks and returned to India, in 1856. Four years later Elizabeth, her second daughter, married Mr. Harding and returned to India. In 1870 Anna, the fourth daughter, married Mr. Park and went to the same field in India. In 1875 Dr. William Ballantine followed as a missionary physician. Henry, the elder son, a graduate of Amherst, has been, for nearly twenty years, in India in mercantile agencies which leads him to travel over that eastern world. Miss Fairbanks, grandchild of Mrs. Ballantine, is now teacher of the "Girl's School" at Ahmednagar; Henry Fairbanks, brother of Miss Fairbanks, has two years more at Yale Theological Seminary. He expects to go as a missionary where his parents and grandparents labored. The mother's utterance, in the agony of her buried hopes, as she saw the remains of her deceased husband sink beneath the Atlantic waves, "It does not seem possible that I can ever return to the scene of my missionary labors again; *but this one thing I will do*, I will educate my children and send them back" is more than fulfilled. It reaches on to the grandchildren and why should it not be perpetuated to the third and fourth generation and on and on till the missionary work shall be needed no more? when there shall be no need of one saying to another "Know thou the Lord; for all shall know Him from the least even unto the greatest." John Ballantine is a minister in Dorchester, Mass., and Julia married a minister, Rev. Mr. Greenwood, who is settled at Windsor, Vt. Mr. and Mrs. Park are now in this country. He is pastor of the Howard Avenue church, New Haven, Conn.

WILLIAM WOOD.

The question has been asked "What led you to become a missionary?" There may be some here to-day asking the same question. During the great and precious revival of religion in 1831 I was one of the converts and with some fifty others united with the church in the autumn of that year at the age of thirteen. In the written narrative of my Christian experience I find these words: "If I know my own heart I have a desire to serve God the rest of my days." The new spiritual life given in the conversion of the soul was the germ which led me to be a missionary, that germ was quickened into life when I was received into membership with a church of which its members were warm-hearted, earnest and devoted. The atmosphere was one of love. Fervid were the prayers offered. Our pastor, Mr. Scales, was alive to the work of teaching us the first principles of the Christian faith. The members of the church were helpers in the same direction; by them we were encouraged to take a part in prayer-meetings, testifying what God had done for us, and to lead in prayer. The young members of the church were encouraged to have prayer-meetings of their own in the different neighborhoods of the town, to pray for one another, and for their young friends and urge them to come to Christ. We went by two and two from house to house till all the families of the town were visited. What is this but missionary work and what were we but missionaries? Mr. Scales early brought before our minds the subject of the Christian ministry as our life work, and in time a class of six young brethren of our church was formed and entered upon a course of study for preaching the gospel. I was one of the six. George Champion of Colchester, Conn., where Mr. Scales formerly preached, decided about this time to be a missionary to the Zulus of South Africa. He visited Mr. Scales and preached here. Amos Sutton, a Baptist missionary, also preached in our church. Later Elizabeth Darling left us for India as a missionary. By these living examples of consecration to mission work my attention was directed to the same work. Academy and college days passed by; six years of hard study and the want of funds led me to teach for a time. In 1844 I entered Union Theological Seminary of New York. The missionary spirit was there. Howland was under appointment, three members of my class had decided to enter the field. George Bowen, who went with me to India, was one of the three. A missionary revival continued all the time. In the vacation of the first year, while employed as colporter of the American Tract Society in Clinton County, N. Y., I came to the decision to became a missionary to foreign lands and on my return to the Seminary I entered the "Missionary Band." I finished my studies in 1847, was ordained in this house July 8th of the same year, was united in marriage on the 11th with Lucy Maria Lawrence of Groton, Mass., sailed from Boston on the 31st for Bombay, and after nearly a six months' voyage arrived there Jan. 19, 1848. Our first work was the study of the language, which is Marathi. Toward the end of the year I made my first effort at preaching. The leadings of Providence sent us to Satara, an interior station, 168 miles south-west of Bombay. Satara had then a population of 32,000, the capital of a state, of the same name, of a million and a quarter of pagans. Others had labored here at times, but it was not considered a station of our mission till we went there in 1849. There was no mission house, no house for us to live in, no chapel and no school-house. In due season we built a good mission house, beautiful for situation, a chapel and school-room were also soon built. Death is busy in a tropical climate. We had not been in our new mission three months before he entered and took from it the light of my home. With two little boys I labored there alone till a brother missionary and his wife with two little daughters came to live with me. In less than two years that dear missionary sister ended her work. For nearly a year I was thus left to be father and mother to my own little boys and to three little daughters of my brother missionary. At the close of the year 1854 I took my little boys to this country and returned to India in 1856. In 1857 the Sepoy mutiny came on, a hundred thousand Sepoys were in arms, and for a long time it seemed that every Christian in India, European and native, would be cut off. We were mercifully cared for by our Heavenly Father. Our work went on again till 1859 when I was again left alone. For two years and a half *alone* I held on, sowing in tears; not tired of the work, but tired and breaking down in health. Again I came to America for health. In 1865 again I returned to the work. I cannot in the time allotted tell of the work. I employed native Christian men and women to help me in preaching and teaching and putting into circulation far and wide the Word of God, in the Scriptures, in books and tracts and in every feasible method which offered to bring truth to the people. You may ask, "why did you give up the work?" For the same reason that the soldier is removed from the battle-field, not dead but wounded and unfit for service. The place for him is in the hospital or his home among friends. Disabled I left the work for others to do. Since I left India I am thankful to say that the work is going on with increased interest. The church has increased in numbers and in strength and is now self-supporting. They have an excellent native pastor, good schools for Christian and heathen children and a force of native helpers employed in evangelistic work. "All the way my Father led me." He led me to that distant land; He led me back; He led me to my present beautiful home in the country town of North Branford, Conn. In a small way I am pursuing the avocation of my youth—a tiller of the soil. For eleven years I have been a quasi pastor. I have a large Bible class and find enough Christian work to occupy my time. I feel that I am a missionary still, and I expect to be a missionary so long as I live.

Henniker, June 7, 1884.

HISTORICAL ADDRESS.

BY J. M. R. EATON, *pastor of the church for* 17 *years.*

A church is a formally organized body of Christian believers worshiping together. This defines the word church according to our ideas of it. There are many, however, who would not accept this definition, who speak of *the* church, meaning thereby all bodies of believers who observe the same rites and acknowledge the same ecclesiastical authority; such as *the Presbyterian church*. But this method of subjecting all believers to some definite form of government is post-apostolic. It is something which grew into existence gradually, originating, doubtless, not from any Scriptural instruction or suggestion, but from the nature of the civil government which, at the time, swayed its sceptre over both Jews and Gentiles. We prefer, however, to go back of all this human machinery to the time when the gospel, preached by the apostles, was proving itself the power of God and the wisdom of God to many who believed in various parts of the empire and were gathered into churches. In accordance with this we read that Paul and Silas went through Syria and Cilicia confirming the *churches*. We have the authority of Christ to the same effect, who taught the apostle John to write, "He that hath an ear, let him hear what the Spirit saith unto the *churches*." It is of one of these churches, amenable to no human authority for its forms of worship, in doctrinal belief built upon the foundation of prophets and apostles, Jesus Christ, himself, being the chief corner stone, and animated by the spirit of the living God, that we are about to speak.

Christian churches, adopting essentially the same form of government, and the same great underlying principles of revealed truth, will often develope different traits of character, occasioned by various circumstances. But while this may be true their leading characteristics will be alike because wrought out by the inworking of the same divine Spirit and through the same God-given revelation.

Time and circumstances will allow us to give but a very brief history of the Congregational church of Henniker.

The territory, originally known as No. 6, was granted to certain persons July 16, 1752, but was not incorporated till Nov. 10, 1768, when it received its name in honor of John Henniker, Esq., of London, Eng. Among other conditions on which this tract of land was granted we find the following, that "within the space of three years from the time of their being admitted, they [the grantees] build and finish a convenient meeting-house for the public worship of God and settle a learned Orthodox minister." This territory was to be laid out into shares and one of the shares was reserved "for the first minister of the gospel who shall be regularly settled on the said tract of land, and continue there during his life, or until he be regularly dismissed;" and "that one other of said shares be for the use of the ministry there forever." And "that one of the lots of the share for the use of the ministry be laid out in the most convenient place for building a meeting-house." The committee appointed to locate this house of worship reported, as early as Oct. 22, 1766, a lot of land near the end of the road leading down the north side of Craney hill; but the town took no action which resulted in the building of the house till March 26, 1770, when they voted to build a house 30 feet long by 20 feet wide, and allowed *twenty dollars* for the carrying of this vote into effect. This was the next year after the church was organized. And the committee, to whom was entrusted the work of erecting the house, seem to have proceeded forthwith to a partial accomplishment of it. The walls were built of logs, and while yet roofless the people gathered here, under the vault of heaven, to worship God with a feeling somewhat akin, we may well imagine, to that of the Psalmist: "How amiable are thy tabernacles, O Lord of hosts."

The church had already been organized. This event occurred June 7, 1769. The record is as follows: "On the 7th of

June, 1769, a church of Christ was embodied in the presence and by the direction of an ecclesiastical council. The members of the church then embodied were as follows: Jacob Rice, pastor elect; Timothy Ross, Ezekiel Smith, Josiah Ward, Ebenezer Harthorn, Thomas Howlet, William Pressbury, Silas Barns and Charles Whitcomb."

The church thus organized adopted the following

COVENANT.

"We, whose names are underwritten, apprehending ourselves hereunto called, do now, in the presence of God, profess to choose the Lord Jehovah to be our God; to fear him in love and serve him in truth with all our hearts, giving up ourselves to be his, and in all things to be at his disposal and sole direction, that we may hold communion with him as members of his mystical body, according to his revealed will, to our lives' end. We also bind ourselves to bring up the children which God has graciously, or shall give us, in the knowledge and fear of God, according to our abilities, and in the use of the orthodox catechisms, that the true religion may be maintained in our families while we live, and among those who may live when we are dead and gone. We further promise to keep close to the truths of Christ, and with affection in our hearts to endeavor to defend it against all opposers as God shall at any time call us thereunto. And that we may do this we resolve to use the Scriptures as our platform (whereby we may discern the mind of Christ) and not the new found inventions of men. We also engage to have a careful inspection over our own hearts, and endeavor, by virtue of the death of Christ, a mortification of all our sinful frames and disorderly affections whereby we may be drawn from the living God. We moreover oblige ourselves faithfully to improve our abilities and opportunities in worshiping God according to the institutions of Christ for his church under gospel administration, to give renewed attention to the word of God, pray to him and sing his praise and hold communion with him in both the seals, Baptism and the Lord's Supper. We also promise that we will peaceably submit to the discipline of Christ's church, obeying them who have the rule over us in the Lord. We also bind ourselves to walk in fellowship with one another, as a particular church of Christ, and in love towards others, endeavoring mutual edification, visiting, exhorting and comforting as occasion serveth, warning any brother or sister that offend, not divulging private offences, but heedfully following Christ's precepts for church dealing in Matthew 18:15, 16, 17, willingly forgiving all who manifest to the judgment of charity that they truly repent of all their miscarriages."

From the time the church was organized till Oct. 20, 1777, its work is not recorded; but from that date till Sept. 4, 1795, the records were made by Rev. Mr. Rice, at the close of which he says, over his own signature, "The above written is a true copy of the church records."

I have searched the records with all diligence and do not find any account of additions to the church during this period. At one church meeting the question was raised whether a certain man was a member, which, at an adjourned meeting, was decided in the affirmative; and from this time on till 1802 no admission is recorded, although certain persons, without naming them, are said to have been propounded for admission. And there are forty-six names, in the list of members, after the organization of the church and previous to the settlement of Rev. Moses Sawyer, in 1802, none of which appear upon the records as having been received, although the names of some of them are recorded as having been placed on committees at various times. A private communication informs me that there were six females who united with the church at its organization, whose names are not certainly ascertained. How the facts concerning these, or the forty-six referred to above, have been ascertained, whether by tradition or from papers which have not fallen into my hands I am not able to say; I think, however, by tradition.

We cannot just yet take leave of that little band of June 7, 1769. For about a year whatever meetings they had must have been held in private houses. Mr. Rice, who was installed as their pastor the same day on which they were organized into a church, was with them, interested in all that interested them. They were scattered over this territory, working hard and amid many privations during the week, and on the Sabbath day, with no highways leading to the place of worship, wending their way thither as best they could. But at length the day arrives when the place of public worship is inclosed with logs; and, roofless though it be, they enter it with praise and thanksgiving. Look for a moment at the spectacle which they present! The light of heaven shines not upon them through stained windows, but falls upon them unobstructed from the open sky. Their reverend pastor stands behind no elegantly wrought pulpit. They sit not in cushioned pews. What solemn stillness pervades the assembly as God's presence and blessing are invoked! With what devotion and uplifting of soul they sing his praise without the help of organ or quartette! With what hungering and thirsting for the bread and water of life do they hang upon the lips of their young pastor as he unfolds to them the word of God! With what patience—no, no, with what gladness do they sit upon these hard benches till the close of an all-day service, and then, with a benediction, return to their isolated homes! Let imagination fill out the picture thus meagrely drawn, for we must not linger here.

With the addition of a few more dollars a roof was placed upon this house, which continued to be the place of worship for ten years, with no glass windows, no heating apparatus, except such as is brought in foot stoves from the homes of the worshipers; absolutely nothing, in the *circumstances*, which here and now would be tolerated for a single hour. And yet, through cold and heat, tempest and calm, rain and snow, and two protracted services on the Sabbath day, the word of the Lord had free course and was glorified in this log sanctuary. and perhaps no ten years of the church's history has had a greater influence in moulding the character of the people of this town. It was in this house that the citizens gathered during the national struggle for liberty, and listened to the patriotic, soul-stirring, courage inspiring words of their pastor, and from here numbers of them went forth to the field of strife. Of some it is said that, Cincinatus like, the next morning after the alarm from Lexington, they left their oxen in the yoke, or, unyoking, left them to shirk for themselves, and left for the war. But we are in danger of lingering here too long, for the torch of an incendiary is already kindled, and on the morning following the *dark day*, May 20, 1780, the ancestors of some here may have been heard to say, with some qualifications, "Our holy and our beautiful house, where our fathers praised thee, is burnt up with fire, and all our pleasant things are laid waste."

During the six or seven years that followed, religious meetings were held in private dwellings, and the church, several members of which had been in the war, had become somewhat *militant* in ecclesiastical matters. Efforts were made to secure another place of worship, and votes were passed by the town looking to the accomplishment of this object; but the most difficult question to be settled was where to locate the house. The center of the territory seems to have been in the neighborhood of the first church building; and there are always some who esteem it almost a sacrilege to abandon a spot thus made sacred. Others preferred some other part of the center lot. The diversity of opinion was so great and unyielding that the matter was referred to a committe out of town, who reported in favor of the location where the house was afterwards built. The town accepted this report, but afterwards set it aside, and appealed to the Legislature, then sitting at Exeter, to help them out of their trouble by the appointment of a disinterested committee of three from the neighboring towns. The committee was appointed, their decision accepted, and by the aid of *three barrels of rum*, at a cost of 12£, 5 s., 1½ p., the frame of the house now standing on the south side of the river was raised in the autumn of 1786. It was not till the next spring that the house was enclosed. Meetings were held in it during this year, but it was not till 1788 that the town took measures to put in the pews. For a very accurate and minute description of this house I must refer you to the History of Henniker.

After Mr. Rice's dismission, and while he continued to supply the pulpit, a period of twenty years, many candidates were heard, and several calls extended to men to settle with them in the gospel ministry. But there was a lack of harmony between the church and town. It will be remembered that the condition on which the territory was granted was that the ministry should be of the orthodox persuasion. Such were the men whom a large portion of the church desired to settle; and the reason why the town did not accept them is probably to be found in a difference of views upon religious subjects between this portion of the church and a majority of the voters of the town.

Aug. 12, 1801, the town voted to settle Rev. Moses Sawyer;

but on the 9th of the following December reconsidered this vote which led to the formation of a new society, called "The Calvinistic Congregational Society of Henniker." As the members of this society were in the minority of the voters in the town, and so of the owners of the house of worship, by this step they sacrificed their interest in the house. The record of this transaction reads as follows: "Considering that we have long been destitute of a pastor, that our utmost exertions to obtain such a blessing have ever been disappointed by divisions in the town, and seeing not the least prospect that the town of Henniker will ever settle a faithful minister of Christ, with any promising harmony; therefore, *Voted*, That we feel ourselves called in Providence to give up our connection with said town, in regard to a minister, and unite with such other inhabitants as will join with us, in a Calvinistic Society for the support of public worship." By this decisive vote the knot was cut which held the church to a body of men who had no sympathy with them on a subject of the most vital character. This took place Dec. 14, 1801. I find no record of any formal organization of a Calvinistic church. Whether such an organization was effected, the record of which is lost, or the members thus leaving the old church did not consider a new organization necessary, I am not able to say. There is a record of the renewal of the church confession of faith, Nov. 11, 1802, and this may have been consider as the origin of the new organization.

The members of the Congregational Society, being a majority, of course owned the house of worship. But Dec. 8, 1802, they "*Voted*, That the Calvinistic Society, so called, should have the liberty of going into the meeting-house on the Sabbath when the town did not wish for said house." But as the town occupied the house whenever they had a supply for the pulpit, the new church was obliged to resort to private houses, school-houses, and barns so often that they decided to build another house, which they did, locating it but a few rods from where this house now stands, dedicating it in 1805. Concerning this house I find a record, dated Aug. 23, 1833: "This morning, between three and four o'clock, the meeting-house, which the church had occupied for public worship thirty years, was discovered on fire; and the house with all that was in it, viz., Bibles, testaments, hymn books, Sabbath-school library, stoves, etc., was consumed, with communion ware." Now, for the fourth time, there was a houseless church. Measures were soon taken, however, to erect another house of worship, and in one year and four days, Aug. 27, 1834, this house, in which we are now assembled, echoed with glad anthems at the dedication service. The tongue of the first church bell in town, speaking in the name of heaven, called the people together on this eventful and interesting occasion. The house has been remodeled and improved at different times, until, to-day, through artistic skill and much manual labor, in convenience and beauty, it is all that could be desired; and may the kind providence which has guarded it hitherto long preserve it to this worshiping congregation.

Thus far we have directed thought to the gathering and housing of the church. The beginning was small and hedged about with difficulties. From that time till now often the clouds have been heavy and the darkness dense; then light has broken in to inspire courage and give hope, so that obstacles have been overcome, and prosperity has crowned faithful effort. And to-day, on the *one hundred and fifteenth* anniversary of the gathering of the church, contrasting the present with the past, you come together with glad hearts to praise Him who has led you hitherto.

PASTORS.

But we must not forget that a Christian church needs something besides a house in which to worship God. History abundantly confirms the truth of the statement, that a church thus left would soon become extinct; or at the best, lead but a sickly life. It has already been said that one of the original members of this church was a preacher of the gospel. Rev. Jacob Rice was here to gather this church, and the same council that organized the church consecrated him to the work of the ministry and installed him as their first pastor. He was a native of Northboro', Mass., and a graduate of Harvard College. He devoted himself faithfully to his work for about four years, when a severe fit of sickness so impaired his health that he was ever afterwards an invalid, and unable fully to meet the de-

mands of his office. Some were disposed to complain on this
account; and from this time forward he was much tried by
physical infirmities and the dissatisfaction which existed among
his people. He continued pastor, however, till Feb. 20, 1782,
when, by an ecclesiastical council, he was dismissed. He continued for about 20 years occasionally to supply the pulpit. He
seems to have been a man of positive theological views, which
he did not fail to preach. Doubtless in this, quite as much as
in his feeble health, we must find the occasion of the opposition which prevailed somewhat extensively in the town against
him. He had a kind and generous heart towards his people,
but he also had a heart loyal to Him who had called him into
the ministry; and we may well suppose that he labored in the
spirit of the apostles when they said : "Whether it be right in
the sight of God to harken unto you more than unto God, judge
ye."

Being an educated and professional man, standing at the
fountain head of the stream of influences that spread over this
territory, we should naturally expect that he would impress
himself largely upon the people. Accordingly we read, in addition to his strictly religious work, that "to him more than to
any other one person is the town indebted for the school system
which has been in vogue in the town for upwards of a century."
On leaving here Mr. Rice removed to Brownfield, Me., to take
charge of a church, then recently organized, where he died
Feb. 1, 1824, at the age of 83 years. We are told that two
weeks previous to this event he walked six miles, preached
twice and walked home again; and that, on the day of his
death, while preaching his morning sermon, he was seized with
apoplexy, carried to his house, where, at three o'clock, the master, whom he had served in the ministry more than 54 years,
call him to his reward.

Rev. Moses Sawyer was the next pastor of this church. He
was a native of South Hampton, N. H., born March 11, 1776,
graduated at Dartmouth College 1798, where he gave the
philosophical oration, showing him to have been one of the first
scholars in his class. He read theology with Rev. Asa Burton,
of Thetford, Vt. He was a fine classical scholar, a thorough

and well read divine, and a pious and devoted Christian. August 12, 1801, the town voted, 54 to 33, a call to him to settle with them in the gospel ministry. September 11, of the same year, a church meeting was held in the school house, near by, and voted unanimously to give him this call. It seems probable that the members of the church were not all present. December 9, following, the town held another meeting, more fully attended, and reconsidered the vote of August 12, declaring against his settlement by 90 to 66. It was at this point that Mr. Sawyer's friends withdrew and decided upon a new organization; and December 31, 1801, at a special meeting, the church voted unanimously to invite Mr. Sawyer to become their pastor; and he was installed May 26, 1802. This was effected by an ecclesiastical council, of which Rev. Samuel Wood was moderator, and Rev. Walter Harris, scribe. The installation services took place in Mr. Whitman's barn, near by, the east scaffold serving for a pulpit, from which Rev. Mr. Worcester preached the sermon. But it was not done without an effort on the part of the town to prevent it, for they delegated a number of their most influential citizens to represent to the council the feeling that existed in opposition to this movement.

After the settlement of Mr. Sawyer, the town made an effort to keep up their organization, but never succeeded in the settlement of another pastor. They had preaching occasionally, but finally agreed to allow Mr. Sawyer and his people the use of the house, when it was not otherwise wanted. But when it was wanted the new congregation repaired to some schoolhouse or barn; and wherever they went the blessing of the Lord went with them. They entered their new house of worship, as has already been said, in 1805. Many of those who were opposed to Mr. Sawyer, were gradually won to his support by his impartial treatment, Christian courtesy, exemplary life, and honest presentation of the truths of the gospel, as he understood them. He was dismissed from the pastorate March 29, 1826, and April 9, preached a farewell sermon from the text: "For we are laborers together with God." It must have been in the spirit of these words that he labored so successfully in harmonizing the conflicting elements which he found here at the beginning of his ministry, and held his position for the space of nearly twenty-four years, the longest pastorate in the history of the church. "He was a laborous student always bringing beaten oil into the sanctuary. He aimed to explain to the people the great doctrines of the gospel. He lived and acted, prayed and preached, apparently with the sacredness of his office in view, and with an ardent love of souls in his heart. It was never said that, in all his intercourse with his people, he ever uttered a saying, or did an act, that had a tendancy to bring reproach on the ministry. He was fearless in his defense of the truth, and yet all his conduct was marked with prudence. The cause of God prospered under his ministry." His dismission from this place gave his nervous system a shock from which he never recovered. After leaving here he preached in Searborough, Me., in Gloucester and Saugus, Mass., and died in Ipswich, Mass., of paralysis, Aug. 26, 1847, aged 71, having been in the ministry forty-five years.

Rev. Jacob Scales was the *third* pastor of this church. It appears from the history of the town that his father, also a minister, as early as 1760, resided in this town for a few months and built the first log cabin erected in the territory. He was pastor of the church in Hopkinton, although he preached here occasionally. Jacob was born in Freeport, Me., March 7, 1788. August 27, 1817, he delivered the Latin salutatory oration on the occasion of his graduation at Dartmouth College, which shows the high rank of his scholarship. Three years later he finished his theological course at Andover, and at once became pastor of the Congregational church at Colchester, Ct., where he labored till he received a call from this church, which was voted him Dec. 11, 1826. A few years previous to this, for some reason, there had been formed in town a new religious society, by members seceding from the Calvinistic Society, and calling themselves the Congregational Society. After some efforts to maintain preaching they united with this church and religious society in extending a call to Mr. Scales, and he was installed here Jan. 17, 1827, and dismissed March 1, 1839. Rev. Dr. Justin Edwards, of Andover, Mass., preached the installation sermon, it is said with woollen mittens on his hands. Doubtless he kept himself comfortable while the large congregation shivered in their seats. O the blessing of the modern heating apparatus, if there is not too much of it, and provided always that the pure air of heaven be not shut out! Mr. Scales' ministry here was remarkably successful, measuring it by the accessions to the church. 224 were received during his ministry. He was a man of positive views, and had a positive way of expressing them. Such a man would natually have positive friends and, very possibly, positive enemies. There seems to have sprung up a division among the people, causing no little unpleasantness among themselves, and leading eventually to his dismission, after a pastorate of a little more than twelve years. After leaving here he was settle over the church at Plainfield, remaining there till his death, Oct. 16, 1873, aged 85. Four days previous to this while in the pulpit he was taken suddenly ill, carried to his home, and died the Thursday following. In a little more than two years from the dismission of Mr. Scales, with great unanimity the church extended seven calls to as many men to settle with them in the ministry, all but the last of which were declined. It would appear from such a record that a great degree of harmony had been restored among the members of the church.

The seventh call, unanimous, given July 12, 1841, invited Eden B. Foster to the pastorate, which he accepted, and Aug. 18, he was ordained and installed over the church. The sermon was preached by his uncle, Rev. Amos Foster, of Putney, Vt. Mr. Foster was dismissed Jan. 7, 1847.. This was done after an ineffectual effort to retain him. The feeling of the church in view of his leaving is best expressed in their own language: *"Resolved*, that we exceedingly regret that our beloved pastor, Rev. E. B. Foster, should feel it his duty to ask a dismission from this church; and that it will be almost an irreparable loss; but after much prayer and meditation, we feel it our duty to grant it." The dismissing council say, "that the principal reasons for his request were protracted ill-health and pecuniary embarrassment. The council rejoice that nothing exists, or has at any time existed, to interrupt the harmony and tenderness between the parties here concerned."

Mr. Foster was born in Hanover, N. H., May 26, 1813, the eldest of eleven children, ten of whom were sons. Seven of these received a college education, six of whom entered the ministry. He graduated from Dartmouth College, having pursued his studies there amid many difficulties, among which were sickness and lack of funds. The latter may have been the cause of the former. In his effort not to be burdened with a troublesome debt he boarded himself, living on the most meagre fare. His own testimony is "it is my firm belief that if I had never boarded myself an hour, I should have gained ten years of life which have now been lost through ill-health and despondency." In this way his studies were interrupted to such an extent that his standing in his class was far from being satisfactory to himself. This was the judgment of a despeptic. In some branches of study some of his classmates undoubtedly did excel him, but surely not in all. A classmate and most intimate friend, Hon. James Barrett, of Rutland, Vt., writes thus of him. The day of his graduation was very warm. "Foster's part came about the middle of the afternoon session. The house was densely crowded with a sweltering, tired, uneasy and noisy audience. Little or no attention had been accorded to several preceding speakers, their voices even being mainly inaudible on account of the noise, almost hubbub, throughout the house. Foster was announced. He advanced from the side entrance towards the center of the stage, tall and finely proportioned in figure, dignified and graceful in bearing, solemn and impressive in countenance, wearing the silk robe of those days. As he appeared, and was advancing, a hush in the confusion was obvious, which increased as he approached and bowed to the president, and still more increased as he turned and bowed to the audience. His theme was 'The Eloquence of Expiring Nations'. His first sentence was 'Death, himself, is eloquent.' When he had uttered it, with his deep, rich and commanding voice, with a countenance and bearing that helped to the subduing effect, every sound but the voice of the speaker was hushed to the silence, as it were, of death itself, and that silence continued till he had disappeared from the stage, and still continued till the next speaker was called." The same writer continues: "In all my now long life, in almost annual attendance on commencements of colleges, in more than forty years in courts as lawyer and judge, in the mean time an attendant on sermons, lectures, platform and stump speeches, uttered by all grades, from the highest downward, I have never witnessed such an overmastering effect produced by a speaker upon his audience." Rufus Choate pronounced it the most eloquent performance of the kind that he ever heard.

After a year and a half at Andover Seminary, in Jan. 1840, his health again broke down, and here ended his theological studies preparatory for his future work. After teaching for a time he began his life work of about forty years in the ministry with this church. What has already been said shows the esteem in which he was held here, and the deep and unfeigned regret felt by his people at the necessity of his leaving them. After leaving this place he had four pastorates: one of four and a half years at Pelham, this state; one over the John Street church, Lowell, Mass., of eight and a half years; one at West Springfield, Mass., of four and a half years, and a second time at Lowell, John Street, of sixteen years, where he died April 11, 1882, at the aged of nearly 69 years.

Measured by years his life was not long, but by the work accomplished, longer than that of most men who die of old age. No one acquainted with his habits of study, or listening to his fervid utterances, could reasonably anticipate aught else but that his vital forces would burn out, consuming the body while yet the mind was like the fiery stead, ready for the race course, but held in by bit and bridle. O how delightful to linger the entire hour upon the character of such a man!

Rev. Richard T. Searl was installed the *fifth* pastor of the church, Dec. 1, 1847, and dismissed March 20, 1850. His parents resided in this town from 1820 to 1827. The date and place of Richard's birth, I am not able to give, but probably he was born in New Rowley, Mass., and not long before his parents removed to this town, so that his childhood must have been spent on the north side of Craney Hill. He graduated at Union College, Schenectady, N. Y., in 1832, and at Andover Theological Seminary in 1841, where he was a resident licentiate some years, preaching as he had opportunity. He was ordained at Middleton, Mass., where he had a pastorate of about two and a half years, when he was called to this church. After leaving here he labored with the churches in Marblehead and New Marlboro', Mass., Harwinton and Thomaston Conn., Liverpool, N. Y., Thetford and Windsor, Vt. He died at Danvers, Mass., in 1878, his age being not far from sixty years. My acquaintance with him began on entering the Theological Seminary, in 1841. My impression of him is that he was an able sermonizer, unwilling to lay by his manuscript till he had done his utmost to make it a finished production. This may have been one cause of his frequent removals. The sermon at his installation in this place was preached by Rev. Daniel J. Noyes, of the South church, in Concord.

February 26, 1851, Rev. J. M. R. Eaton was installed the sixth pastor of the church. He was born in Fitchburg, Mass., October 15, 1814, graduated at Amherst College 1841, and at the Andover Theological Seminary, 1844. He went at once to Clintonville, Mass., where he was ordained January 9, 1845. Leaving there in 1847, he was pastor of the church in Shirley three years. He commenced preaching in this place November 3, 1850, was installed February 26, 1851, Rev. E. W. Bullard of Fitchburg, preaching the sermon ; and was dismissed June 2, 1868, a pastorate of between seventeen and eighteen years, being longer than that of any other except that of Mr. Sawyer. His health was so much impaired that he was unable for a time to take charge of another parish. After this, for about seven years, he supplied the church in Medfield, Mass., leaving there July, 1876, and is now residing in Fitchburg. During his pastorate here 88 names were added to the church roll, only one of which was stricken off by excommunicaction. During the same period 67 names were underscored, showing that they had passed from the earthly to the heavenly life. The pastor was called to sit in twenty-six councils. He administered the rite of baptism sixty-two times ; attended one hundred and ninety-two funerals of persons who died in town, besides a large number of those who were brought here for burial, and a very large number in the neighboring towns. He solemnized nintyeight marriages; delivered about fifteen hundred sermons, besides speaking at conference meetings from one to six times a week. He put upon record his greatful remembrance of your invaluable cooperation in the social religious meetings; your promptness in meeting all pecuniary obligations; and your unceasing kindness to himself and family. On resigning his place here the church invited him to withdraw his resignation, which request however was not granted. When assembled, "The council advise that, in view of the enfeebled health of Mr. Eaton and his absolute need of rest and freedom from responsibility, the pastoral relation be dissolved. While reaching this result, we desire to express our deepest regret at the departure from among us of a brother who commands in so eminent a degree our confidence, respect and affection; and who has so unweariedly and successfully labored for the good of those committed to his care. For the church we can express no better wish than that they may receive another pastor who will labor as affectionately and wisely for their good as he who has for seventeen years past served them."

Sept. 1, 1870, Rev. S. S. Morrill was installed the seventh pastor, the sermon being preached by Rev. F. D. Ayer, of Concord. Aug. 18, 1873, at his own request, because of impaired health, he was dismissed from the pastorate. He was born at Danville, Vt., Dec. 24, 1832. He graduated at Dartmouth college in 1855, and studied theology at Andover and Chicago, graduating in 1859. May 12, 1859, he was ordained and installed pastor of the Congregational church at Malden, Ill. During the civil war he was hospital chaplain at Mound City, Ill., where he lost his health which he never fully recovered. Returning East he preached some time at Hillsboro' Bridge, from which place he came to Henniker. After leaving here he had a short pastorate at Harvard, Mass., but was obliged to leave on account of his health. In 1877 he removed to Amherst, Mass., to educate his children; but the next year, his health still failing, he went to his native place in Vermont where he died May 2, 1878, at the aged of 45 years. He possessed a strong intellect and good executive ability, but labored under the disadvantage of poor health during most of his public ministry.

Nov. 21, 1873, the church authorized their executive committee to secure the services of Rev. George H. Morss, with the expectation of settling him as their pastor. Mr. Morss occupied the pulpit nearly three years, but was not installed over the church.

Rev. John H. Hoffman, the eighth and present pastor, was born in Lyndon, Vt., June 10, 1847, graduated at Bates College, Me., 1874, and at Bangor Theological Seminary in 1877. He was ordained in this place Aug. 21, 1877, Prof. William M. Barber of Bangor preaching the sermon. He was installed as pastor June 7, 1878, Rev. C. A. Stone, of Hopkinton, preaching the sermon.

It will be proper here to speak of those who have been members of this church, and became ministers of the gospel.

Jacob C. Goss was born June 4, 1794. He graduated from Dartmouth College in 1820 and at the Andover Theological Seminary three years later. His first year in the ministry was spent in the employ of the Young Men's Missionary Society of Charleston, S. C. In 1824 he was ordained pastor of the First Congregational church at Topsham, Me., serving them seven years. In 1835 he was installed over the church in Sanford, Me., where he remained till 1843 and then was dismissed at his own request. In 1850 he was settled over the church in Wells, Me. Retiring from this field of labor, because of impaired health, he removed to Concord, N. H., in 1853, where he resided until his death, which occurred April 22, 1860. During these years of his residence at Concord he supplied pulpits occasionally, laboring for some time at Randolph Centre Vt. Twelve days before his death he occupied the pulpit at Fisherville, where he took a violent cold which resulted fatally. Mr. Goss possessed a strong mind which was thoroughly disciplined. His theological views were eminently scriptural. His method of presenting truth was unambiguous. His hearers knew what he believed and why he believed it. A "Thus saith the Lord" had greater weight with him than the wisest sayings of uninspired authors.

Parker Pillsbury was born Sept. 22, 1809. Without obtaining a collegiate education, he devoted four years to the study of theology, the fourth year at Andover; and having been licensed to preach the gospel he was engaged to supply the pulpit at Loudon, N. H., for one year. About this time the cruelties of the system of slavery began more especially to be manifest in the mobs and murders of those who had the courage to rebuke them. In 1840 Mr. Pillsbury turned aside from the work of the ministry, and devoted his pen and tongue to the not difficult task of proving slavery to be the "sum of all villanies," but the most difficult work of wiping it out. In it, however, he never faltered, till by the pen of the President and the sword of the nation death came to the system, and life to its subjects. Since that time Mr. Pillsbury has devoted his great powers of intellect and utterance to the work of political and other reforms.

Augustus Berry was born in Concord, N. H., Oct. 7, 1824. He graduated, with high honors, at Amherst College in 1851. During nine years from this date he was engaged in teaching. Five years he was principal of Appleton Academy at Mont Vernon, N H. As a teacher he was eminently successful. Having finished his theological studies at Andover in 1861. he became pastor, the same year, Oct. 30, of the Congregational church at Pelham, N. H., where he still resides. An able, earnest, faithful preacher, beloved by all who know him.

Addison Childs was born in Henniker, Oct. 16, 1821. At the age of 15, he united with the Congregational church in that town. His intellectual faculties developed in a remarkable degree while he was yet very young. He was a leader in debate among his school-mates. It is the testimony of one whose observation is broad, and whose renown is national, that, within the circle of his acquaintance, the native intellect of Mr. Childs had no superior. When yet scarcely 20 years old he took charge of a Methodist academy in Provincetown, Mass., and soon united with the Methodist church in that place. During his two years of teaching he studied with a view to the gospel ministry, and was licensed to preach in 1842. His ministry was brief and interrupted by ill health. He labored in Duxbury, Hyannis and North Bridgewater. Full of zeal and holy ambition he devoted his young manhood to his chosen work, determined to know nothing among his people but Jesus Christ and him crucified. He died Nov. 5, 1844, in the twenty-third year of his age, and the third of his ministry, greatly lamented by the people of his charge, and by a large circle of devoted and admiring friends. Full of faith and the Holy Ghost, for him to live was Christ, and to die, gain.

Nathan Franklin Carter was born in Henniker, Jan. 6, 1830. He graduated at Dartmouth College in 1853, taking a high stand among his class-mates. For eleven years after his graduation he devoted himself, with great fidelity, to the work of teaching, being principal of the high school at Exeter nine years. Seven years previous to closing his labors here he was licensed to preach the gospel; and as health and time permitted, occupied vacant pulpits in the neighborhood. He studied theology at the seminary in Bangor, Me., graduating in 1865. After supplying the pulpit for one year in Pembroke, he preached at North Yarmouth, Me., two years, where he was ordained Dec. 19, 1867. His labors were greatly blessed, resulting in an accession to the church of forty-four members, thirty-four at one time. At his own request he was dismissed April 1, 1869, and in the following August removed to Orfordville, N. H., where he received to the church eighty-four, forty-eight at one time. After leaving Orfordville he preached at Bellows Falls, Vt., and received to the church seventy, thirty-seven at one time. Of these one hundred and ninety-eight, about one hundred and seventy came into the churches on confession of their faith. In 1879 he removed to Quechee, Vt., where he still lives. Here he has received, by confession, nineteen members. This record justifies the remark that Mr. Carter has devoted himself, with great fidelity and earnestness, to the work of preaching the gospel. While he rejoices in the fruit of his labor, he gives to God all the glory.

It may be added here that Mr. Carter is the inventor of the "Rotary Library Reference Table," an ornamental and useful piece of furniture for the office or study of professional men.

DEACONS.

Ebenezer Harthorn and William Presbury were elected deacons at the organization of the church. They both died in 1814, having served the church forty-five years.

In July, 1802, David Clough and Daniel Rice were elected. The former died in 1819 and the latter in 1821, having served in their office about sixteen and one half and eighteen and one half years.

July, 1817, William C. Woodbury and George Connor were elected, and served, the former till 1822, and the latter till 1830.

In 1822 Nathaniel Cogswell was appointed to the office and died in office in 1836.

Josiah Childs and Oliver Pillsbury were chosen in 1831. The former held the office thirty-one years, falling asleep in 1863, and the latter twenty-five years, dying in 1857. Most of these were relieved of the active duties of the office some time before they died.

Horace Childs and Worcester Hathorn were elected in 1855. Dea. Hathorn died in 1880. I find this minute against his name: "No ordinary Christian, forty-eight years a member, twenty-five years deacon." "The righteous shall be in everlasting remembrance." Concerning the character and work of the last four of these beloved brethren it would afford me much pleasure to enlarge; men of sterling worth, godly men, helpers together with one another, with their pastors, with the church, true standard bearers, filling the office of a deacon well. All but one have passed to their reward; of the *one* may it long be said, he liveth, a pillar in the church, a bright and shining light.

In 1883 S. Q. A. Newton, Levi S. Connor and S. W. Carter were constituted deacons.

Thus far the church is organized, housed and officered. But the church itself does not yet stand before us. O for the gift to present the thing of life that it has been in this community. Let imagination picture a community as large as this, for as long a time, and without a church from the beginning, and lay it down by the side of this, and then study the contrasts. Civil government has done something, education much; and yet the contrast remains. But neither government nor schools would have been what they have been, had there been no church. Let us then, as briefly as possibly, sketch the work of the church.

The church has been Congregational in its polity, from the

beginning. At its organization it entered into a solemn covenant one with another. It adopted the Scriptures as its rule of faith and practice, without formulating them into a brief and definite creed. Yet the doctrines usually found in the creeds of evangelical churches were doubtless preached here from the first, and generally accepted by the members of the church. I say *generally*, for it is quite probable that some had come into the church without even professing to have become Christians, for the sake of having their children baptized. In the early history of New Hampshire churches, what is called the *Half-way Covenant*, was somewhat extensively adopted. According to its principles, those who wished to have their children baptized, could be received as members, but not to all the privileges of the church. They were debarred from the communion table. It appears from the records that this church adopted this method of receiving members. October 15, 1795, a council was convened here for the purpose of advising in a case of discipline, and the church requested their advise respecting the propriety of using the half-way covenant. In the following January the church "voted that, from this time forward, no persons shall be received into this church upon the Half-way covenant; but, that those who shall hereafter be admitted, shall come to full communion." While this would not weed out such as had already been admitted, it would tend to keep out, in the future, unworthy members. This step was doubtless seen to be necessary in the practical workings of the church. But little spiritual prosperity had been enjoyed. During the first third of a century, or down to the time of Mr. Sawyer's settlement, only fifty-five persons are known to have belonged to the church; and how many of these came in on the Half-way covenant system is not known. During the first year of Mr. Sawyer's ministry the church formulated their religious belief into eighteen articles, which continued to be read on the admission of members during another third of a century, or until 1835. At this date, and during the ministry of Mr. Scales, a revision of this creed, and without much alteration, was adopted, and at the same time, the covenant renewed. Thirty-seven years later, during the ministry of Mr. Morrill, the church voted to adopt a revised manuel. During all these years essentially the same religious views have been preached and believed.

The records show abundant evidence of a constant effort not only to preserve their ancient faith undiluted, but also to watch over the morals of its members. In the early years many complaints were made of persons walking disorderly; and such cases were followed up till a satisfaction was obtained. Many times delinquents confessed their faults; sometimes, persisting in a course judged wrong by the church, they were cut off from its privileges. Intemperance was often the cause of discipline, intoxicating drinks being everywhere in use. The fellowship of the church has been withdrawn from forty-one of its members. The records afford abundant proof that very much labor was bestowed in nearly all these cases to secure compliance with covenant vows; and in most cases names were dropped, not because of any immorality in the life, but because members had taken themselves away from the fellowship of their brethren.

The work of the church would not be fairly represented without some notice of its efforts in the temperance reform. Intoxicants were freely used a century ago. We have already learned that it took three barrels of rum to raise the frame of the meeting house on the south side of the river. The thought is too deep for us, the back-look too dark, to undertake to solve the problem, how much was required to finish and dedicate it. There must have been a reformation, at least in the case of some of the workmen, before the next house was built, as we are told that one of them, standing upon one foot on a gilded ball, raised six feet above the bell deck, turned himself completely round, demonstrating to the crowd below that his head was steady and his nerve strong. Coming down to the time of the settlement of Mr. Scales, we find this additional testimony. The council that settled him, on the day previous to the event, passed the following resolution: "WHEREAS, intoxicating liquors have in several cases been dispensed with at the entertainment of ecclesiastical councils, and it is understood that the committee of arrangements in this place intend to pursue a similar course,"—all honor to the committee—"this council would express their cordial approbation of it, and their earnest desire that as laudable a practice may become universal." All honor to the council! It will be remembered that Dr. Edwards, the apostle of temperance, was a member of this council, and his "woolen mittens" were a good substitute for the accustomed stimulant. This was in 1827. Who were these men that so nobly stood forth in favor of reform, this committee of arrangements? We are glad to be able to answer the inquiry: Dea. Nathaniel Cogswell, Josiah Childs, Oliver Pillsbury, Steven Searle and Jacob Peters. We should naturally expect that a work thus inaugurated would go forward, and so it did; for eight years later the church "solemnly and explicitly entered into covenant with God, and with one another," that they would abstain "from the use of ardent spirits as a drink." This language may seem tame in this day of pledges to abstain from everything that can intoxicate. But it may be that the former pledge required greater self-denial at that time than the latter at the present time. It requires no stretch of charity to hope that the church of to-day is a unit on this vital subject of temperance.

The church also has a history on the slavery question. As early as 1841 the subject was brought prominently before them; and the next year they adopted resolutions embodying their views. At a meeting of churches in Concord in 1843 Mr. Foster reports: "The injured slave has not been forgotton. A monthly concert of prayer for his deliverance, and for the deliverance of the country from the awful sin of oppression, has been instituted, and attended by increasing numbers, and with augmented solicitude and fervency." But on this subject there was not perfect unanimity. While all would gladly have seen the shackles of the slave broken, some would have it done in one way and some in another. The sixth pastor remembers well the diversity of opinion and of feeling prevaling among the members of the church, and his own possibly too hopeful method of securing perfect harmony by preaching from the text: "I hear that there be divisions among you; and I partly believe it." But be this as it may, I think I never knew a church more harmonious than this became upon this subject. Occasionally a ripple would appear which might easily have resulted in disaster, had not a merciful providence watched over us. The pastor was told that the church had decided that no slaveholder would be permitted to occupy the pulpit, and ordered his course accordingly. On one occasion such a man appeared in the congregation, but of course was not invited into the pulpit. One dear brother felt grieved by this, and suggested to his pastor that he ought to have a mind of his own, and not be bound by any such church action. But grace triumphed, peace reigned, and the pastor had no warmer friends than those who, if anybody, would naturally be offended by his course. But in regard to this action of the church, the records have been searched in vain to find any allusion to it; and probably no such minute was ever entered, if any such resolution was ever passed. But the whole subject of slavery, which vexed the churches of the land so many years, was long since buried, beyond the possibility of a resurrection, in the vast and dreadful grave dug by the civil war. The church from the beginning, has been loyal to the country. Several of the original members were in the war of the Revolution. Few have been in the more recent wars; but church members gave up freely their sons to service and to death. During the Civil War this house witnessed many sad scenes in which the solemn funeral service was performed in connection with the burial of brave men who laid down their lives for the life of the country.

We must not fail to speak of the work of the church in obedience to the Savior's ascending command: "Go ye into all the world, and preach the gospel to every creature." Very early contributions were made to the various missionary organizations. The sixth pastor was installed in Feb., 1851. About three months later I find the following entry: "*Voted*, that Deacons Childs and Pillsbury, together with the pastor, be a committee to report a plan for systematic beneficence." The next month "*Voted*, to recommit the report presented by the committee, 19th ult., to be modified and presented at the next meeting." July 21th, *Voted* to accept and adopt the report of committee touching systematic beneficence." Dec. 15th of the same year "Church organized a Religious Charitable Society, according to constitution adopted July 21," and elected brethren to fill its various offices. For years afterwards a list of all contributors, of the sums contributed, and to what specific objects, was kept; showing the number of cheerful givers to have been very large. During the 33 years, since 1851, between $11,000 and $12,000 have been contributed to benevolent objects, besides very many valuable boxes and barrels of clothing. While during the same period about $40,000 have been expended upon church work at home.

This subject cannot be pursued, neither do we feel at liberty to dismiss it without mentioning one fact showing the reputation of the church on this subject of christian beneficence. At one time the several conferences of the State made an effort to found, each one, a scholarship in Dartmouth College. To secure this end committees were appointed to apportion to each church the amount they would be expected to contribute. For the Merrimack County Conference a prominent business man, and a doctor of divinity, residing at the Capital, solved the problem on a basis which seemed satisfactory to themselves, and sent out the result to the churches. To this church was assigned a sum four times as large as that assigned to a neighboring church whose membership was nearly twice as large as the membership of this church. When asked for reasons, this church was told that the assessments were made on the probabilities of securing the different amounts, judging by the known habits of the churches on this subject of contributions. It is quite natural to inquire why the difference in this respect? Let us then turn to the history of the church and see if we can answer the quession. I know of no more probable cause than that this church has been so largely represented on missionary ground. Both sons and daughters of the church have labored in both the home and foreign field. As many as eight have devoted themselves to this work. Of all these I cannot speak particularly. Suffice it to say that William Wood, having united with this church in 1831, after graduating at Dartmouth College and Union Theological Seminary, was ordained in this house as a missionary af the A. B. C. F. M., in whose service at Satara and Amednaggar, India, he spent a quarter of a century, and only retired because of enfeebled health. Elizabeth Darling united with the church in 1832, and, graduating at Miss Grant's Seminary in Ipswich, Mass., was married to Rev. Henry Ballantine; and May 16, 1835, sailed for India, giving nearly 30 years to the missionary cause; and retired from it only when her husband required rest from labor. In 1864, on their homeward passage, he died and was buried in the waters of the Mediterranean sea. Standing there upon the deck of the Steamer, her heart rent with terrible anguish, this now sainted woman said: "It does not seem possible that I can ever return to the scene of my missionary labors again, but this one thing I will do,—I will educate my children, and send them back to carry on the work left unfinished." Three of her four daughters were married to missionaries and returned to India. One of these rests from her labors, leaving a daughter to carry on the work in the missionary field, another is still in India, the third has returned to this country, the wife at present of a city pastor; the only remaining daughter is the wife of a clergyman. One of her sons has been a missionary physician in India, but is at present pursuing theological studies preparatory for the gospel ministry; another is pastor of a church in Boston. She herself passed to her reward from Amherst, Mass., in 1874. I think the question is easily answered why this church is so much interested in the cause of missions. And besides the missionaries, the church has given several of her sons to the work of the ministry, and of her daughters to become wives of clergymen; and sons and daughters have distinguished themselves as educators, in professional life, and as authors. One would have to look far to find richer poetry, or more perfect oratory than have flowed from the pens and lips of members of this church.

The work of the church in connection with the Sunday school has been of an especially interesting character. But as this has been so ably and faithfully digested and written by another, it is not necessary to repeat it here. For 70 years the work has been in progress, giving precept upon precept, precept upon precept; line upon line, line upon line; here a little and there a little; and the fruits have been most manifest and very precious. It has indeed been the nursery of the church into which have been transplanted very many whose religious life began in connection with the study of the word of God in this institution. The church has not confined its efforts to those usually worshipping with them, but has gone into other communities, and, with no little self-denial, sought to bless them.

While a Congregational church, in an important sense, is a unit, standing by itself, yet it is far from being an independent, isolated body. It has duties as well as privileges which call it abroad in the interest of other churches. And in the fulfilment of these obligations, this church has had a large experience. The first record which I find, calling this church to meet in council abroad, is dated Nov. 6, 1803, to assist in an ordination in Groton, and at the same date, to assist in organizing a church in Bradford. The church has been invited to sit in seventy-nine councils abroad, one third of these, lacking one, was during the sixth pastorate. As the records are imperfect, probably this does not measure the work of the church in this particular department. It has also borne its full measure of responsibility in local and state conferences.

The church has generally been faithful in the performance of Christian ordinances. I find it recorded of Ezekiel Smith, whose name stands third on the list of the original members, that, Jan. 3, 1768, the year before the church was organized, he with his wife, riding upon the same horse, carried their infant child, less than a year old,. to Westboro', Mass., to have him baptized. I also find that Mr. Scales baptized some more than 200 children, many of them by families, when their parents came into the church. Feb. 24, 1839, he made a record in which he stated that there are four children of one sister in the church whose husband refuses to have them baptized; and that there are four other unbaptized children of as many mothers, members of the church, but whose husbands are not. With these exceptions, he says: "I believe there is no child of any member of the church, who is six months old, and has not been baptized." When this statement was given to the public nearly thirty years ago, it was added by the pastor: "The neglect of infant baptism and of family worship is scarcely known among us." During the eleven following years, embracing the pastorate of Mr. Foster and Mr. Searle, only seven baptisms of children are recorded. The sixth pastor baptized forty-one children. And in the sixteen years since his dismission, I find a record of only ten infant baptisms. A very natural inference is that either children are not given to believing parents, or believing parents do not give their children to the Lord in this ordinance.

Thus I have endeavored, with no little effort, to unravel the necessarily mixed, and somewhat confused, and often defective records of this church, and to present them in a logical, that is to say, in this case, a chronological order for your more convenient use. Perfect arrangement, or entire freedom from error is not claimed. It cannot be expected that you will be as much interested in the result as I have been in working it out; for I have seemed to live through this more than century, and to be not merely a witness, but almost a participant in what has transpired. I have been, as it were, a worshiper in the roofless log house; have been present at the raising of the second church edifice, which required all the strength of the community, somewhat nerved to the work by an evil *spirit*, to throw up the massive timbers; have listened to the voice of the preacher as it came down from yonder scaffold; have held my breath while gazing with the astonished crowd up to that workman standing on one foot upon the gilded ball, sympathizing with Butler:

"If any yet be so foolhardy,
T"expose themselves to vain jeopardy,
If they come wounded off and lame,
No honor's got by such a main;"

have wondered how, in the burning of this same house, the stoves were consumed together with bibles and hymn books; without the aid of imagination, for nearly eighteen years, have come up to this house of prayer with the people of God to whom I gave my best earthly love, and to part with whom cost a sacrific, the record of which is in the book of remembrance and can never be effaced from this undying memory. All these pastors have passed before me, entering upon their work in the freshness of young manhood, with a holy ambition devoting their energies to the building up of this church in its varied interests, most of them retiring in enfeebled health. All of the speaker's predecessors, and his immediate successor, have passed from the earthly to the heavenly employment, and are today associated with many who have become stars in the crown of rejoicing.

I have witnessed your joys at the bridal alter, and in the wider social gatherings; have also stood in more than a hundred of your dwellings, in the midst of weeping circles, where the palor of death rested on the countenance of some loved one, where the hand was palsied, the heart motionless, the lip sealed, the eye shut.

Six hundred and fifty names stand on your register, about three hundred and fifty of which are italicized, emphasizing not so much the fact of death, as of life, *eternal life*.

The present membership is one hundred and eighty.

٢

The Congregational Church,

HENNIKER, N. H.

ORGANIZED JUNE 7, 1769.

MANUAL

OF THE

CONGREGATIONAL CHURCH,

HENNIKER, N. H.,

ADOPTED FEBRUARY, 1872.

"THE FOUNDATION OF GOD STANDETH SURE, HAVING THIS SEAL, THE LORD KNOWETH THEM THAT ARE HIS. AND, LET EVERY ONE THAT NAMETH THE NAME OF CHRIST DEPART FROM INIQUITY."—*2 Tim. 2:19.*

CONCORD, N. H.:
PRINTED BY THE REPUBLICAN PRESS ASSOCIATION.
1872.

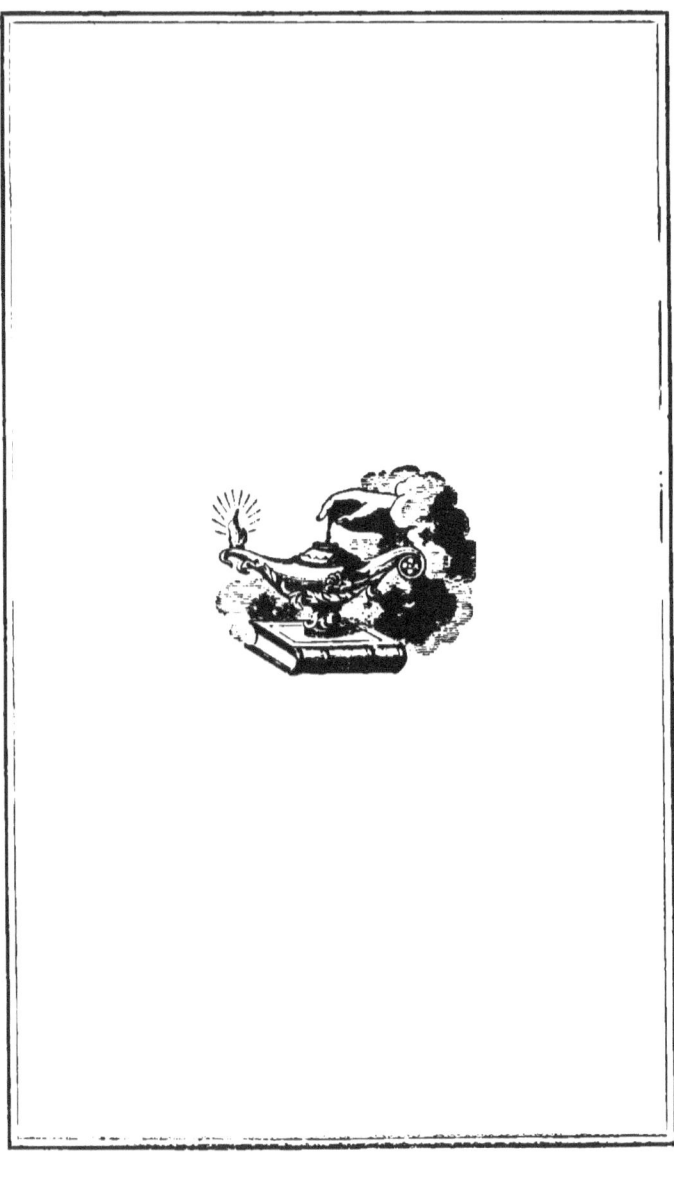

MANUAL

OF THE

CONGREGATIONAL CHURCH.

HISTORICAL SKETCH.

As early as 1748, several persons, inhabitants of Londonderry, associated with view to obtaining a grant of unoccupied land. In 1752 they succeeded, receiving July 16 of that year, a proprietor's right to what is now the township of Henniker.

The French war coming on, no settlement was made till 1761. During that year James Peters located with his family, and the next year other families followed. The township charter was granted Nov. 10, 1768, by George III, through Gov. John Wentworth, and at that time there were thirty families within its limits. The name is said to have been given by Gov. Wentworth in honor of a London friend of his who bore the same.

During the summer of 1768, individuals had subscribed to hire Jacob Rice to preach the gospel among them; and June 7, 1769, a council was called to assist in organizing a church. At that time the present Congregational church was organized and Mr. Rice ordained its pastor, the town assuming his support.

The church adopted no Confession of Faith at its organization, but covenanted to be "guided in all things by the Holy Scriptures."

Fifteen years afterwards it voted to accept "that part of the Cambridge Platform, entitled Admission of Members," and two years later it adopted five Rules of Discipline, of which no record is preserved. On Nov. 11, 1802, the church adopted a carefully prepared Confession of Faith, which, as revised in 1835, and again in 1872, still continues to be the symbol of its belief. This church practised the half way covenant, so called, till 1795.

The first building for religious worship—a log house 20 by 30 feet—was erected in 1770, and occupied ten years, when it was burned. After this, till 1786, the town was without any house of worship. That year it voted to build one "40 by 60 feet, with two porches, on the centre lot." At a subsequent meeting it voted to add five feet to its length; and this house, when completed, was occupied till 1802. In that year, differences arising respecting the settlement of a pastor, it was closed to the church, and has since been occupied chiefly as a town house.

Another house of worship was erected in another part of the village the same year, and occupied till August 23, 1833, when it was burned with all its contents; and, through a defective title, the ground upon which it stood reverted to the original owners.

Not to be overcome by adversities, the church and society connected with it immediately secured a new location, and began to build the fourth house of worship. This was completed, and dedicated Aug. 27, 1834. It still continues to be the Church Home.

ADMISSION OF MEMBERS.

[The persons will present themselves before the pulpit, and the minister will address those to be admitted by profession, as follows:]

Jesus says, If any man will come after me, let him deny himself, and take up his cross, and follow me. For whosoever will save his life shall lose it; and whosoever will lose his life for my sake shall find it. Whosoever therefore shall confess me before men, him will I confess also before my Father which is in heaven. But whosoever shall deny me before men, him will I also deny before my Father which is in heaven.* In obedience to Christ's command, and as an expression of your love and devotion to him, you now desire to make public profession of your faith, and to enter into covenant with this church in doctrine, in fellowship, and in duty.

Dearly beloved, we trust you feel the solemnity and blessedness of this confession of discipleship to Jesus, the Christ. May the blessing of God the Father rest upon you, that it may be to the praise of the glory of his grace: for by grace ye are saved through faith. Let a sense of your own weakness teach you dependence upon divine strength for ability to keep these solemn vows; and your faith in the promises assure you that He who hath begun a good work in you will perform it until the day of Jesus Christ.

* Matt. 16:24 and 10:32.

[The minister will address those admitted by letter as follows:]

You have already made public confession of your discipleship to Jesus Christ, and been received into another branch of the Household of Faith. A change of residence has cast your lot among us; and that you may still have the fellowship of believers and be most truly a servant of the Master, you now seek admission to this communion. You come to us bearing letters of commendation from the communion you leave; and we joyfully receive you, only asking that you assent to our Confession of Faith, that you renew your covenant with your Saviour, and enter heartily into these new relations.

You will now attend to the articles which this church has adopted as its

CONFESSION OF FAITH.

We believe there is only one true God, a spirit, infinite in every natural and moral perfection.

We believe that the Scriptures of the Old and New Testaments were given by inspiration of God; that they contain a complete and harmonious system of religious truth, and are the only infallible rule of religious faith and practice.

We believe God is revealed in the Scriptures as Father, Son, and Holy Spirit; and that these three are one.

We believe God governs all things according to his eternal and infinitely wise purpose, securing his own glory and the greatest good of the universe; and in perfect consistency with his hatred of sin, the free agency of man, and the importance of the use of means.

We believe the law of God that requires holiness of heart and life is benevolent and wise, and is binding as a rule of duty upon all mankind.

We believe God created man holy, and that he fell from this state by sinning against God; that the race is now destitute of holiness, and so continues until quickened by the Holy Spirit.

We believe that, according to the prediction of God, the Son has come in the flesh, and made an atonement sufficient for all mankind; that God can now consistently, and will, pardon all who repent and believe on the Lord Jesus Christ.

We believe in the necessity of the new birth, and that it is a moral change produced by the Holy Spirit operating on the mind through the truth, in which the person freely turns from all known sin.

We believe the sinner's justification is of free grace, and through faith in the atonement of Christ.

We believe all true Christians are God's chosen people, and that, though free to fall, they will be kept by the power of God through faith unto salvation.

We believe that watchfulness over the life, the study of the Scriptures, a conscientious attendance upon public and private worship, together with the steady practice of righteousness, truth, sincerity, and charity toward others, of sobriety, chastity, and temperance toward ourselves, are indispensable Christian duties.

We believe in the visible church of Christ on earth; and that it consists of those who publicly profess their faith in him, and covenant together to walk in the ordinances of his gospel.

We believe in the divine appointment of the Christian Sabbath, the gospel ministry, and the sacraments of the New Testament,—Baptism and the Lord's Supper; that Baptism is to be administerd only to believers and their households; and the Lord's Supper only to those in regular standing in some evangelical church.

We believe human probation ends at death, and that there is a day appointed in which Christ will raise the dead, and judge the world in righteousness; that those who die impenitent will go away into everlasting punishment, but the righteous into life eternal.

Do you confess this as your Christian belief?

[Persons will assent by bowing; then baptism will be administered to such as have never been baptized; after which the minister will address those baptized in childhood, as follows:]

Through the faith of Christian parents you have already received baptism. You do now acknowledge as valid the ordinance of baptism administered to you in childhood, by which your parents gave you up in solemn consecration to God? You do here publicly assume all the obligations as well as privileges that baptism signifies, and now, by your own choice, ratify and complete that membership in Christ which parental faith and love begun for you?

You will now assent to the

COVENANT.

In the presence of angels and men, you solemnly avow the Lord Jehovah to be you God, the object of your supreme affection.

You accept the Lord Jesus Christ as your Saviour; the Holy Spirit as your comforter; and the Bible as your rule of life.

You heartily consecrate yourself to God and his service in an everlasting covenant.

You purpose, by divine grace, to obey his commandments; to give diligent attention to his word and ordinances, to family and secret prayer, and to the observance of the Sabbath.

You design to seek the honor of his name, and the interest of his kingdom; and, denying all ungodliness and every worldly lust, to live soberly, righteously, and godly in the world.

You also covenant to walk with this church of Christ in Christian love, fellowship, and faithfulness; to coöperate in its measures for the support of the gospel; to contribute of your means according to your ability; and in all things to seek its peace and prosperity while you continue a member of it.

In humble dependence upon divine grace for needful help in keeping these vows, do you thus covenant?

[The church will rise, and the minister will continue as follows:]

Most affectionately now do we, the members of this church, in the name of Jesus Christ, welcome you to this communion, and to all the blessed privileges of children in our Father's house. We break with you this bread of life. We share with you this cup of blessing. We ask your aid in turning to our Master the hearts of the children of men. We covenant with you to hold your peace and welfare dear to us. We promise gladly to render our offices of love; and, so far as we are able, to seek your growth in grace, your sweet experience of Christ's love, and your perfect meetness for the heavenly home.

And now, dearly beloved, we commend you unto the Father of our Lord Jesus Christ, of whom the whole family in heaven and earth is named; that he would grant you, according to the riches of his glory, to be strengthened with might by his Spirit in the inner man; that Christ may dwell in your hearts by faith, and ye be filled with all the fulness of God. And unto him that is able to keep you from falling, and to present you faultless before the presence of his glory with exceeding joy, to the only wise God, our Saviour, be glory and majesty, dominion and power, both now and ever. Amen.*

* Eph. 3:15; Jude, 24th verse.

BAPTISM OF CHILDREN.

[Parents desiring to have their children baptised are requested to bring them, if convenient, on Communion sabbath, at the opening of the afternoon service. They are also requested to give the pastor suitable notice, together with the child's name and date of birth.]

In presenting this child for baptism, you profess your faith in the covenant made by God with Abraham, ratified by Christ, and perpetuated under the Christian dispensation. As Abraham, the father of the faithful, entered into covenant with God, and his seed after him, so do you now covenant with him in the dedication of this child to his service. You hereby engage to be faithful to your parental relations; to pray for and with this child; to instruct him (her) in the doctrines and duties of our holy religion; to set an example of godliness before him (her); and to endeavor, by all the means of divine appointment, relying much upon the gracious influences of the Holy Spirit, to prepare him (her) for full admission to the visible church on earth, and the church triumphant in heaven.

Jesus said, Suffer the little children to come unto me, and forbid them not; for of such is the kingdom of God. And he took them up in his arms, put his hands upon them, and blessed them.*

BAPTISM.

BAPTISMAL CHANT.

PRAYER.

* Mark 10: 14, 16.

STANDING RULES.

[Let all things be done decently and in order. 1 Cor. 14:40.]

I. POLITY.

This, as a Congregational church, receives all its authority from the word of God. It is competent to exercise that authority independent of any other ecclesiastical body, so far as relates to its internal organization, the administration of gospel ordinances, the choice of its officers, and the admission, discipline, and removal of its members. Its relation to other churches is that of fellowship and communion, according to established Congregational principles.

II. OFFICERS.

The permanent officers of the church are a pastor and two or more deacons.

In addition to these, the church will choose annually a clerk, a treasurer, and a committee of examination.

III. DUTIES.

The pastor shall be a member of this church, and when present act as moderator at its meetings.

The treasurer will have charge of all money received by contribution or otherwise, disburse the same as directed by the church, and make an annual report in writing.

The clerk will keep the records of the church, and make an annual report; in which report he shall give the number of members, the number and manner of additions and removals during the year, together with a list of non-resident members and any information respecting them he may deem it important to communicate.

The committee will examine candidates for admission to the church, and have the special care of its discipline.

IV. MEMBERSHIP.

Persons desiring to unite with the church by profession of faith will give the committee satisfactory evidence of their conversion, and be recommended by them to the church. They will also present before the church a written or verbal statement of their Christian experience, and be voted upon one by one.

All candidates for admission by profession will stand propounded two weeks; and, if they have been approved by vote of the church at a regular meeting, they may be received at the following communion by assenting to the Confession of Faith and Covenant.

Persons desiring to unite by letter will pass their letters to the pastor, who will examine the case, and, if no objection is found, recommend the person to the church for its action; when received, they will, at the first convenient opportunity, publicly assent to the Articles of Faith and Covenant of the church.

Members who are absent for one year or more are expected to take letters to other churches, or give the clerk good reasons for not doing so.

Members of other Congregational churches, who may desire to commune with us for more than one year, are expected to unite with us unless there are special reasons for delay.

V. DISCIPLINE.

The occasions of discipline are of two kinds: private, as wrong done to an individual; and public, as wrong done to the church by immoral conduct, or cherished disbelief, or continued neglect of covenant obligations. The rules given by Christ in Matthew 18 : 15–17, are to be followed by members of the church in cases of private offence; and the spirit of these rules must govern all disciplinary action of the church.

When any member is guilty of a public offence, it is the duty of any other member who has knowledge of the facts, to seek, according to the preceding rules, to lead him to repentance; and when neglected by others it shall be the special duty of the examining committee.

The extent of discipline is private reproof, public admonition, temporary suspension from church privileges, or excommunication, according to the nature of the offence.

VI. CHURCH NOTICES.

Regular contributions are made to such benevolent objects as the church, from time to time, may select.

The annual meeting for hearing reports, choosing officers, &c., is held on the last Thursday of the year, and in connection with the prayer-meeting of that day.

The Sacrament of the Lord's Supper is administered on the afternoon of the first Sabbath in January, March, May, July, September, and November.

The preparatory lecture is on the Thursday preceding each communion Sabbath, at 2 o'clock.

A Church prayer and conference meeting is held on Thursday of each week.

A monthly concert of prayer for missions is held on the first Sabbath evening of each month.

The Sabbath services commence at 10: 30 A. M., from the first of November to the first of April, and at 11 A. M., during the remainder of the year.

CATALOGUE OF OFFICERS AND MEMBERS.

PASTORS.

Rev. Jacob Rice, ordained June 7, 1769; dismissed Feb. 20, 1782.
Rev. Moses Sawyer, ordained May 26, 1802; dismissed March 29, 1826.
Rev. Jacob Scales, installed Jan. 17, 1827; dismissed March 1, 1839.
Rev. Eden B. Foster, D. D., ordained Aug. 17, 1841; dismissed Jun. 7, 1847.
Rev. Richard T. Searle, installed Nov. 30, 1847; dismissed March 20, 1850.
Rev. J. M. R. Eaton, installed Feb. 25, 1851; dismissed June 2, 1868.
Rev. S. S. Morrill, installed Sept. 1, 1870.

DEACONS.

Ebenezer Hathorn, chosen June 7, 1769; died Feb. 5, 1814.
William Pressbury, chosen June 7, 1769; died ——
David Clough, chosen July 23, 1802; died Jan. 2, 1819.
Daniel Rice, chosen July 23, 1802; died Jan. 15, 1821.
William C. Woodbury, chosen July 16, 1817; resigned Nov. 19, 1822.
George Connor, chosen July 16, 1817; excommunicated Jan. 23, 1830.
Nathaniel Cogswell, chosen Nov. 18, 1822; died July 17, 1836.
Josiah Childs, chosen Dec. 5, 1831; died Feb. 1, 1863.
Oliver Pillsbury, chosen Dec. 5. 1831; died Feb. 27, 1857.
Horace Childs, chosen Feb 19, 1855.
Worcester Hathorn, chosen Feb. 19, 1855.

LIST OF MEMBERS,

WITH DATE AND MANNER OF RECEPTION AND REMOVAL.

P   Admitted by profession.   Ex. Removed by excommunication.
L.   Admitted by letter.   } Connects husband and wife.
*   Removed by death.
Dis. Removed by dismission.   ( ) Encloses husband's name.

ORIGINAL MEMBERS.

Silas Barnes	*	Timothy Ross	*
Ebenezer Hathorn	*	Josiah Ward	*
Thomas Howlet	*	Charles Whitcomb	*
William Pressbury	*	Ezekiel Smith	*

Jacob Rice (pastor elect) Dis. Oct. 29, 1822

ADDED MEMBERS REMOVED.

Received.   *Removed.*

Received			Name	Husband/Note	Removed
Feb.	12, 1832	P	Abbott Clarissa	(Stephen Leverett — Vermont)	Dis. Nov. 17, 1834
May	10, 1812	P	Abbott Sarah	(Dyer)	Dis. March 23, 1834
			Adams Sally	(Benj. Hoyt)	Dis. Dec. 23, 1810
Nov.	11, 1838	P	Alley Mary B.	(Joshua Alley / Henry Parkinson)	*
			Amsden Joseph }		*
			Amsden Abigail }		*
Nov.	8, 1816	P	Atkinson James V. }		Dis. Sept. 30, 1827
Aug.	11, 1816	P	Atkinson Jane }		Dis. Sept. 2, 1827
Feb.	11, 1855	P	Bacon Louisa	(A. D. L. F. Connor)	*
			Bailey Elizabeth		*
July	14, 1822	L	Bailey Abigail		*
Aug.	12, 1838	P	Ballard Maria C.	(Capt. Jas. Ballard / Rev. Jacob Scales)	Dis. Nov. 10, 1839
			Barnes Elizabeth	(Silas)	*
Nov.	14, 1824	P	Bartlett Caroline L.	(John S.)	Dis. Nov. 11, 1842
Nov.	13, 1842	P	Berry Rev. Augustus		Dis. Dec. 11, 1864
Nov.	9, 1831	P	Blanchard Mehitable	(Nathan)	*

Received.					Removed.
April 29, 1835	P	Blanchard Nathan }			Dis. Dec. 19, 1861
May 8, 1857	L	Blanchard Abigail }			Dis. Dec. 19, 1861
May 9, 1858	P	Blanchard S. Garland			Dis. Dec. 19, 1861
		Bowman Francis			*
		Bowman Prudence	(Jonas)		
Nov. 3, 1816	P	Bowman Azubah	(Francis Bowman jr.) (Dea. Asa Abbott)		*
Aug. 12, 1838	P	Bowman Ruth A.	(Levi Bowman) (William Cheney)		*
May 10, 1829	L	Brooks Elmira	(Paschal)		*
Aug. 8, 1858	P	Brown Mary J.			Ex. Feb. 8, 1863
July 29, 1810	P	Butler Sally	(Silas Whitney)		Ex. July 20, 1835
		Campbell Abigail	(Annas)		*
Aug. 21, 1843	P	Carter Rev. N. F.			Dis. April 11, 1858
March 24, 1859	P	Carter William			*
Feb. 14, 1830	P	Cate Huldah	(Varney Wardwell)		Dis. Nov. 12, 1837
		Childs Solomon			*
		Childs Patty			*
		Childs Aaron			*
March 25, 1810	P	Childs Dea. Josiah }			*
March 25, 1810	P	Childs Abigail }			*
		Childs Patty	(William Eaton)		Dis. Sept. 18, 1803
Aug. 8, 1824	P	Childs Solomon jr.			*
Aug. 8, 1824	L	Childs Lucinda			*
Nov. 13, 1831	P	Childs Josiah jr.			Dis. Jan. 1, 1837
Nov. 13, 1831	P	Childs Rosella	(John Whitney — Edgerton)		Dis. May 10, 1837
Feb. 8, 1835	P	Childs William C.			*
Feb. 21, 1836	P	Childs Addison			*
May 8, 1842	P	Childs Caroline	(John J. Stillman)		Dis. Nov. 15, 1847
Aug. 12, 1839	P	Childs Martha	(Benjamin Colby)		Dis. May 4, 1856
May 8, 1842	P	Childs Julia A.			*
May 14, 1843	P	Childs J. Webster			Dis. July 25, 1850
Aug. 21, 1843	P	Childs Mary E.	(Calvin Lowe)		Dis. April 3, 1854
April 29, 1835	P	Childs S. Austin			Dis. Dec. 27, 1846
Feb. 11, 1849	L	Childs Philena	(Carlos)		*
Jan. 14, 1850	L	Choate Lucy	(Solomon)		*
		Clough Dea. David			*
Aug. 14, 1803	L	Clough Abigail	(Nathaniel)		*
March 25, 1810	P	Clough Benjamin			Dis. Oct. 16, 1814
Aug. 11, 1833	P	Cochrane Mary			*
April 11, 1816	P	Cogswell Hannah	(David)		*
Nov. 3, 1816	P	Cogswell Dea. Nathaniel }			*
Nov. 18, 1827	L	Cogswell Lucy P.			*
Nov. 13, 1831	L	Cogswell Thomas }			Dis. Dec. 18, 1836
Nov. 13, 1831	L	Cogswell Hannah }			*
Nov. 13, 1831	P	Cogswell Jonathan }			Dis. Dec. 18, 1836
Nov. 13, 1831	P	Cogswell Mary D. }			Dis. Dec. 18, 1836
Nov. 10, 1833	P	Cogswell George W. }			Ex. March 20, 1848
Nov. 11, 1838	P	Cogswell Mary L. }			Ex. March 20, 1848
Feb. 8, 1835	L	Cogswell Louisa D.	(Thomas)		Dis. Dec. 18, 1836
Feb. 8, 1835	P	Cogswell Abigail A.	(Benj. Andrews)		*
April 29, 1835	P	Cogswell Abigail P.	(Daniel)		Ex. March 20, 1848
April 29, 1835	P	Cogswell Mary H.	(Charles Choate)		Dis. Oct. 11, 1866
May 11, 1856	P	Cogswell Mary	(Washington)		*
Aug. 8, 1858	P	Cogswell Susan C.	(Geo. K. Moulton)		Dis. Oct. 23, 1859
July 10, 1803	P	Colby Mary	(David)		*
May 12, 1805	P	Colby Sally	(Solomon Newton)		*
Nov. 5, 1818	P	Colby Lydia	(Eliphalet jr.)		*
Feb. 14, 1830	P	Colby Mary			*
June 29, 1830	L	Colby Sarah C.	(Langdon)		Dis. Aug. 7, 1859
Nov. 13, 1831	P	Colby Levi }			Dis. May 4, 1856
Nov. 13, 1831	P	Colby Betsey }			Dis. May 4, 1856

Received.					Removed.
May 13, 1832	P	Colby Lucy	(Samuel Gammel)		Dis. Dec. 9, 1838
May 13, 1832	P	Colby Catherine	(John Crowell)		Dis. Sept. 19, 1842
Feb. 10, 1833	P	Colby Lydia	(Nicholas Robbins)		Dis. Dec. 9, 1838
April 29, 1835	P	Colby Benjamin			Dis. May 4, 1856
April 29, 1835	P	Colby Mary	(Erastus Taylor)		Dis. Jan. 15, 1837
April 29, 1835	P	Colby Levi jr.			Ex. July 17, 1848
May 8, 1836	P	Colby Elizabeth	(Jonathan)		*
May 8, 1842	P	Colby Lucinda	(Charles Conn)		Dis. May 4, 1856
Feb. 11, 1844	P	Colby Joshua H.			*
Aug. 8, 1858	P	Colby Joseph B.			*
Aug. 11, 1861	L	Colby Dea. Nehemiah			*
		Connor Dea. George	}		Ex. Jan. 23, 1830
		Connor Hannah	}		Ex. Jan. 21, 1833
Nov. 25, 1804	L	Connor Susanna	(John T.)		*
April 11, 1816	P	Connor John	}		*
April 11, 1816	P	Connor Mary	}		*
Nov. 13, 1831	P	Connor Abel	}		*
Aug. 14, 1831	L	Connor Martha	}		*
Aug. 14, 1831	L	Connor Susan H.	(William)		*
Feb. 12, 1832	P	Connor Liva	(Solomon Heath)		Dis. Feb. 6, 1840
Aug. 12, 1832	P	Connor Liza			*
Nov. 11, 1838	P	Connor Eunice C.	(E. P. Leach)		Dis. Nov. 9, 1866
Nov. 11, 1838	P	Connor Hannah C.	(P. M. Flanders)		Dis. July 6, 1851
Nov. 10, 1844	P	Cotton Sophronia	(Nathaniel)		Dis. Aug. 30, 1847
May 11, 1834	P	Dale Betsey	(Philip)		*
Feb. 25, 1616	P	Darling Isaac			*
Feb. 12, 1832	P	Darling Geo. A. P.			Dis. June 16, 1834
Feb. 12, 1832	P	Darling Elizabeth	(Henry Ballantine)		Dis. Aug. 10, 1866
Aug. 12, 1832	P	Darling Joshua	}		*
Aug. 11, 1811	P	Darling Mary	}		*
Aug. 11, 1833	P	Darling Susan W.	(Jonathan P.)		Dis. Jan. 25, 1835
April 29, 1835	P	Darling C. P. H.			Ex. April 17, 1848
Aug. 11, 1816	P	Davis Thomas M.	}		Ex. Feb. 21, 1831
Aug. 11, 1816	P	Davis Phebe	}		
Aug. 12, 1832	P	Davis Mary	(John Proctor)		Dis. Sept. 10, 1837
Aug. 9, 1835	P	Davis Wells			Dis. Jan. 14, 1850
March 20, 1803	L	Dimond Ezekiel	}		Dis. April 17, 1808
March 20, 1803	L	Dimond Abigail	}		Dis. April 17, 1808
Aug. 11, 1816	P	Dufer Hannah	(Abel)		*
June 20, 1802	P	Dutton Jeremiah	}		Dis. July 28, 1805
June 20, 1802	P	Dutton Betsey	}		Dis. July 28, 1805
Jan. 2, 1803	P	Euger Sarah	(Joseph)		*
Oct. 27, 1822	P	Eaton Obediah P.			Dis. June 20, 1825
Feb. 8, 1835	P	Eaton Page	}		Dis. Oct. 2, 1853
May 13, 1832	P	Eaton Roxy B.	}		Dis. Oct. 2, 1853
Nov. 14, 1858	P	Eaton Thomas E. W.			Dis. Jan. 8, 1865
Feb. 8, 1835	P	Farmer Silas			*
Nov. 18, 1800	P	Flanders Nancy	(James)		*
May 18, 1828	P	Foster Polly	(Zebulon)		*
April 29, 1835	P	Foster Zebulon			*
Sept. 16, 1841	L	Foster Rev. E. B.	}		Dis. April 15, 1851
Sept. 16, 1841	L	Foster Catherine P.	}		Dis. April 15, 1851
Aug. 3, 1851	P	Foster Caroline F.	(William Folsom)		*
May 8, 1864	P	Foster Julia M.	(Charles Foster) (Orlando Fitts)		*
Nov. 8, 1857	P	Folsom Samuel			*
Nov. 13, 1831	P	Gammel Lydia			*
July 25, 1802	P	Gibson Dinah			*
July 29, 1810	P	Gibson Persis	(Charles Pingree)		Ex. July 2, 1823
Aug. 8, 1824	P	Gibson Lewis	}		*
Aug. 11, 1816	P	Gibson Lucy	}		*
Nov. 11, 1832	P	Gibson Elvira			*
Feb. 8, 1835	P	Gibson Lydia D.	(Nahum Gibson) (John Stewart)		*

Received.					Removed.
April 29, 1835	P	Gibson Susan	(John)		*
Feb. 12, 1832	P	Gordon Mehitable	(Jeremiah Davis / James Ellis)	Ex. Aug. 10, 1837	
Nov. 9, 1834	P	Gordon Lydia	(Jacob)		*
April 29, 1835	P	Gordon Emily K.	(Abram Goldsmith)	Dis. July 15, 1850	
		Goss Ephraim		Ex. Jan. 23, 1830	
		Goss Ruth		*	
July 29, 1810	P	Goss Sally		*	
Feb. 25, 1816	P	Goss Rev. Jacob C.		Dis. Dec. 26, 1824	
Aug. 11, 1816	P	Goss Annas		Ex. Feb. 21, 1831	
Nov. 9, 1834	P	Goss Luther		*	
		Gould Amos		*	
		Gould Mary		*	
Dec. 14, 1817	L	Gould Gertrude	(Elias)	Dis. Oct. 21, 1821	
Feb. 14, 1830	P	Gould Clarissa L.	(Chevey Chase)	Dis. Oct. 18, 1841	
May 13, 1832	P	Gould Elias jr.		*	
Aug. 11, 1811	P	Gould Sally		*	
May 13, 1839	P	Gould Daniel C.		Dis. Feb. 21, 1842	
Feb. 8, 1835	P	Gould Lavinia M.		*	
Aug. 21, 1813	P	Gould Emeline A.	(Gilbert)	*	
Nov. 11, 1838	P	Gove Louisa		*	
Nov. 11, 1838	P	Gove Mary	(Amasa Bryant)	Dis. March 1, 1868	
Nov. 9, 1828	L	Graves Amasa		Dis. Feb. 17, 1840	
Aug. 8, 1824	P	Greenleaf Mary B.	(William)	*	
May 4, 1823	P	Hardy Judith		Dis. April 13, 1828	
		Hathorn Rhoda	(Dea. Ebenezer)	*	
Aug. 14, 1825	P	Hathorn Polly		*	
Nov. 14, 1824	P	Hathorn John jr.		*	
Feb. 10, 1833	P	Hathorn Levi		Dis. ——1844	
May 8, 1836	P	Hathorn Eliza		Dis. April 11, 1852	
Oct. 3, 1802	P	Heath Lois	(Mathias)	*	
Feb. 8, 1818	P	Hill Josiah		Dis. Jan. 14, 1828	
Feb. 8, 1818	P	Hill Abigail		Dis. Sept. 17, 1827	
Nov. 9, 1834	P	Holmes Auna	(Oliver Holmes / Daniel Fuller)	Dis. July 1, 1839	
		Howe Eliakim		*	
		Howe Rebecca		*	
Dec. 6, 1812	L	Howe Phebe	(Ezra)	*	
Aug. 11, 1816	P	Howe Eli		*	
		Howe Lucy	(Otis)	Dis. Nov. 7, 1805	
Aug. 8, 1830	P	Hoyt Betsey J.	(Samuel Sargent)	Ex. July 16, 1832	
Nov. 13, 1831	P	Hoyt Saunders		Dis. May 6, 1842	
Nov. 13, 1831	P	Hoyt Sally		Dis. May 6, 1842	
Nov. 13, 1831	P	Hoyt Emily A.	(Peleg Smith)	Ex. June 13, 1867	
May 14, 1837	P	Johnson Anna S.	(John)	*	
Nov. 3, 1816	P	Jones Susanna		*	
April 12, 1840	P	Kimball Jane	(Phineas)	*	
Nov. 14, 1858	P	Kinsman Hattie F.		Dis. Feb. 8, 1863	
Aug. 11, 1816	P	Kirk John		Dis. July 1, 1839	
Nov. 3, 1816	P	Kirk Dorothy		Dis. July 1, 1839	
Nov. 13, 1831	P	Kirk Thomas		Ex. March 19, 1855	
Nov. 13, 1831	P	Kirk Elizabeth			
Aug. 12, 1832	L	Lancaster Alice	(Jacob)	Dis. Oct. 20, 1834	
Nov. 13, 1831	L	Lewis Nancy		Dis. Nov. 10, 1833	
Sept. 29, 1816	P	Livingston Lucy	(Nathaniel)	*	
Nov. 11, 1832	L	Lowell Sally		*	
Nov. 13, 1836	P	McColley James		Dis. March 21, 1842	
Nov. 13, 1836	L	McColley Sarah		Dis. Nov. 7, 1841	
Aug. 16, 1807	P	Mirick Elizabeth	(William)	*	
Feb. 8, 1835	P	Mirick Lydia	(Moses)	*	
Feb. 25, 1816	P	Moore John		Dis. Sept. 14, 1817	
March 25, 1810	P	Morrill Susanna	(Ephraim)	*	
Nov. 13, 1831	P	Morrill Ephraim jr.		*	

Received.				Removed.
Nov. 13, 1831	P	Morrill Lucy	(Thomas Wallace / Samuel Rolfe)	Ex. Nov. 1, 1866
		Morrison Samuel }		*
		Morrison Margaret }		
Aug. 12, 1804	P	Morrison William {		Dis. June 7, 1840
		Morrison Jane }		Dis. July 14, 1839
Aug. 11, 1816	P	Morrison Dea. Samuel }		Dis. Aug. 31, 1829
April 25, 1824	P	Morrison Betsey }		Dis. Aug. 31, 1828
May 8, 1831	P	Morrison Mary Ann (Rev. J. M. C. Bartley)		*
		Morrison Susanna		
Feb. 12, 1832	P	Morrison Eliza		
Nov. 13, 1831	P	Morse Josiah }		*
Feb. 8, 1835	P	Morse Betsey B. }		*
Nov. 9, 1834	P	Morse Caroline L.	(Josiah Jr.)	*
		Newton Nahum }		*
		Newton Mercy }		*
Aug. 12, 1838	P	Newton Solomon		*
Aug. 24, 1838	P	Newton Catharine		*
Aug. 8, 1824	P	Page Sarah	(Jonathan)	Dis. June 4, 1848
June 20, 1802	P	Parker Alexander		Dis. July 28, 1805
Nov. 11, 1832	P	Patten Mary G. (Dr. Franklin Wallace)		Dis. Mar. 24, 1867
April 29, 1835	P	Patten Nancy		
March 15, 1847	L	Parmenter Mary	(David)	*
Aug. 8, 1802	P	Patterson Susanna	(Joseph)	*
Feb. 12, 1832	P	Patterson William }		Dis. Oct. 21, 1844
Aug. 8, 1824	P	Patterson Francis }		Dis. Oct. 21, 1844
May 13, 1834	P	Patterson Hon. J. W.		Dis. Oct. 24, 1852
March 20, 1803	L	Pearson John }		Dis. Apr. 17, 1808
March 20, 1803	L	Pearson Elizabeth }		Dis. Apr. 17, 1808
Feb. 21, 1836	P	Perkins Elizabeth		*
Nov. 11, 1838	P	Perkins Margaret		*
Nov. 10, 1867	L	Perkins Lucy S.		*
		Peters Sarah	(James)	*
Feb. 23, 1817	P	Peters Jacob }		*
Feb. 23, 1817	P	Peters Anna }		*
May 12, 1822	P	Peters Hannah		*
Nov. 13, 1831	P	Peters Eliza		*
Nov. 11, 1832	P	Peters Sarah E.	(Joseph Colby / C. G. McAlpine)	Dis. Dec. 17, 1865
Aug. 12, 1838	P	Peters Mary C.		*
Aug. 8, 1824	P	Pillsbury Dea. Oliver		*
Aug. 11, 1833	P	Pillsbury Parker		Ex. Nov. 17, 1845
Apr. 29, 1835	P	Pillsbury Oliver jr.		Ex. Apr. 18, 1853
Nov. 11, 1838	P	Pillsbury Eliza J.		Dis. July 18, 1841
Apr. 29, 1835	P	Pillsbury J. Webster		Ex. Nov. 1, 1866
Nov. 13, 1831	P	Pressbury Louisa M. (Wheelock Campbell)		Dis. Apr. 18, 1842.
Apr. 29, 1835	P	Pressbury Maria E.		Ex. Jan. 21, 1839
March 25, 1810	P	Proctor John C.		Dis. July 16, 1815
Dec. 30, 1810	P	Proctor John }		*
Dec. 30, 1810	P	Proctor Edna }		*
Feb. 25, 1816	P	Proctor Rev. David C.		Dis. Feb. 14, 1819
Aug. 10, 1834	L	Proctor Abigail		Dis. Apr. 16, 1837
Aug. 14, 1859	P	Plummer John R. }		Dis. June 22, 1871
Aug. 14, 1859	P	Plummer Harriet P. }		Dis. June 22, 1871
July 29, 1810	P	Putney Lydia	(Thomas)	*
May 18, 1828	P	Putney Sally C.	(Lot Wiggins)	Dis. Apr. 19, 1835
May 13, 1838	P	Putney Mary M.	(Perley)	Dis. June 21, 1840
Feb. 10, 1837	P	Putney Charles G.		Dis. Feb. 9, 1868
Feb. 9, 1834	L	Quimby Jonathan		Dis. Dec. 23, 1838
Aug. 11, 1811	P	Ramsdell Abigail	(Isaac Ramsdell / Francis Withington)	

Received.					Removed.
Nov. 13, 1831	P	Ray Amos }			Ex. March 18, 1833
Feb. 12, 1832	P	Ray Catherine }			*
		Rice Ruth	(Rev. Jacob)		*
Nov. 14, 1830	P	Rice Lucy			*
		Rice Dea. Daniel }			*
		Rice Sarah }			*
Nov. 13, 1831	P	Rice Moses			*
Feb. 12, 1832	P	Rice Levi			*
May 13, 1839	P	Rice Martha	(Elisha)		*
Aug. 21, 1843	P	Rice Maria W.	(Obediah Wilson)		*
		Ross Kesiah	(Timothy)		*
Nov. 13, 1831	P	Rogers Artemas }			Dis. Apr. 21, 1833
Nov. 13, 1831	P	Rogers Lydia }			Dis. Apr. 21, 1833
Nov. 13, 1831	P	Sanborn Dr. Nathan			*
Aug. 29, 1835	P	Sanborn Sarah (Dr. Appleton Sanborn)			Dis. Oct. 17, 1842
Aug. 9, 1835	P	Sanborn Paulina	(James Sargent)		Dis. Sept. 20, 1840
May 8, 1842	P	Sanborn Nathan P.			Dis. Feb. 29, 1852
Feb. 11, 1844	P	Sanborn Geo. G.			Dis. Feb. 24, 1846
Feb. 11, 1855	P	Sanborn Henry M.			Dis. May 9, 1862
Aug. 8, 1858	L	Sanborn Caroline A. (Edward B. S.)			*
March 20, 1803	L	Sargent Lydia	(Ebenezer)		*
Feb. 21, 1836	P	Sargent Betsey }			*
Aug. 13, 1837	P	Sargent Thomas }			*
Apr. 11, 1858	L	Sargent Dea. James }			*
Apr. 11, 1858	L	Sargent Mercy }			*
Aug. 8, 1830	P	Saunders Betsey B.			Dis. Oct. 20, 1834
May 26, 1802	L	Sawyer Rev. Moses }			Dis. May 3, 1826
Dec. 4, 1803	L	Sawyer Fanny }			Dis. Sept. 12, 1831
March 20, 1803	L	Sawyer Edmund }			Dis. Oct. 16, 1814
March 20, 1803	L	Sawyer Mehitable }			
Feb. 12, 1832	P	Sawyer Jacob }			Dis. Nov. 20, 1843
Feb. 12, 1832	P	Sawyer Laura B. }			Dis. Nov. 20, 1843
Apr. 12, 1827	L	Scales Nancy B.	(Rev. Jacob)		*
May 8, 1859	P	Scott Philluda C.	(S. G. Blanchard)		Dis. May 7, 1869
Apr. 15, 1821	L	Searle Dea. Stephen			Dis. Oct. 28, 1827
Aug. 8, 1824	P	Senrle Sarah J.	(Isaac Adams)		Dis. Oct. 28, 1827
Oct. 22, 1848	L	Searle Rev. R. T. }			Dis. Oct. 21, 1866
Oct. 22, 1848	L	Searle Emily A. }			Dis. Oct. 21, 1866
		Smith Ruth	(Ezekiel)		*
		Smith Hannah	(Samuel)		*
May 12, 1805	P	Smith Abigail	(Ezekiel jr.)		Dis. July 29, 1810
July 5, 1807	P	Smith Prudence	(Bezaleel)		*
		Smith Susanna	(Moses)		*
		Smith Betsey			
May 8, 1831	P	Smith Thankful			*
Nov. 13, 1831	P	Smith Mary Ann			*
Nov. 11, 1832	P	Smith Mary	(Bimsley)		*
Apr. 29, 1835	P	Smith Peleg W.			Ex. April 16, 1868
Apr. 29, 1835	P	Smith Rev. Socrates			Dis. Nov. 11, 1842
May 13, 1838	P	Smith Elijah }			Ex. June 13, 1867
May 13, 1838	L	Smith Hannah }			Ex. June 13, 1867
Oct. 11, 1840	L	Smith Sally	(Bezaleel)		*
Aug. 8, 1858	P	Smith Harriet	(Micah Howe)		Dis. May 15, 1862
May 9, 1813	P	Sprague Timothy }			*
Nov. 10, 1811	P	Sprague Azubah }			*
Feb. 21, 1836	P	Stiles Amelia	(Madison Colby)		Dis. July 12, 1840
Dec. 4, 1803	L	Stone Mary	(Thomas)		*
Dec. 8, 1816	P	Temple Rhoda	(Jasper)		Dis. May 21, 1848
Apr. 29, 1835	P	Train Rebecca H.	(Jeremiah Dutton)		Dis. Aug. 3, 1840
Aug. 11, 1833	P	Tucker Hannah	(Ezra)		Dis. Sept. 30, 1866
Apr. 29, 1835	P	Tucker Clarissa P.	(David)		Dis. March 24, 1867
Nov. 13, 1836	L	Tucker Sophronia (Samuel Folsom)			Dis. Sept. 30, 1866
		Wadsworth Samuel			Ex. April 24, 1826

Received.					Removed.
Nov. 3, 1816	P	Wadsworth Joanna	(Bela Butler / Dan Wilson)		*
Aug. 8, 1824	P	Wadsworth Titus V.			Ex. Sept. 19, 1853
Apr. 12, 1827	P	Wadsworth Susan			Dis. July 6, 1855
May 16, 1830	P	Wadsworth Joseph			*
Nov. 13, 1831	P	Wadsworth Dorothy	(Benoni Fuller)		Dis. Feb. 25, 1849
Nov. 13, 1831	P	Wadsworth Betsey S.	(——Warren)		Ex. Nov. 1, 1866
Nov. 13, 1831	P	Wadsworth Olive	(Joseph)		*
Nov. 12, 1843	P	Wadsworth Burton			Ex. April 19, 1858
Nov. 12, 1843	P	Wadsworth Sophia			
Nov. 12, 1843	P	Wadsworth Carlton			Ex. April 19, 1858
	P	Ward Sarah	(Josiah)		*
May 12, 1805	P	Ward Josiah jr.			Dis. July 22, 1810
May 12, 1805	P	Ward Elizabeth			Dis. July 22, 1810
Dec. 30, 1810	P	Wallace Betsey	(Robert Wallace / Jno. Franklin)		Dis. Oct. 21, 1821
May 13, 1838	P	Wallace Jane	(Robert M.)		
Apr. 29, 1835	P	Watkins Helena C.	(Ruggles S.)		Dis. July 20, 1846
		Whitcomb Hannah	(Charles)		*
		Whitcomb Jacob			*
		Whitcomb Olive			*
Nov. 13, 1831	P	Whitcomb Polly	(John)		*
Nov. 13, 1831	P	Whitcomb Laura			*
Nov. 13, 1831	P	Whitcomb Sally M.	(Enoch Coffin)		Dis. Nov. 2, 1834
Nov. 11, 1832	P	Whitcomb Eunice	(Silas)		*
		Whitney Joshua			Ex. Dec. 3, 1832
		Whitney Betsey			Ex. Dec. 3, 1832
May 12, 1805	P	Whitney Hannah	(Abel Connor)		*
Nov. 3, 1816	P	Whitney Stephen			Dis. April 22, 1827
Nov. 13, 1831	P	Whitney Asa			*
Nov. 13, 1831	P	Whitney Lois C.	(Zebulon Foster jr.)		*
Feb. 12, 1832	P	Whitney Alice B.			*
May 13, 1832	P	Whitney Martha	(Asa)		*
Nov. 10, 1833	L	Whitney Lois			*
Nov. 13, 1831	P	Wilkins James			*
Aug. 8, 1858	P	Wilkins B. Jane			*
Aug. 8, 1858	P	Wilkins Mary C.			*
Feb. 22, 1816	L	Wilson Dea. William			*
April 29, 1835	P	Wilson Polly E.	(Samuel)		*
Aug. 8, 1802	P	Withington Rachel			*
May 11, 1806	P	Withington Francis			*
Aug. 12, 1832	P	Withington Francis M.			*
Nov. 14, 1802	P	Withington Hannah			*
Feb. 10, 1805	P	Withington Mary	(Elias)		*
May 14, 1820	P	Withington Cynthia			*
Aug. 8, 1824	P	Withington Laura	(David Clough jr.)		Dis. Sept. 17 1832
May 13, 1832	P	Withington Apphia	(——Emerson)		Ex. June 13, 1867
		Wood Jonathan			Ex. Dec. 3, 1832
		Wood Sarah			
Aug. 14, 1803	L	Wood Elizabeth	(Joseph)		*
Aug. 12, 1804	P	Wood Betsey			*
Aug. 12, 1821	P	Wood Betsey	(James B.)		*
Aug. 8, 1824	P	Wood Levi			Ex. Jan. 23, 1830
Aug. 8, 1824	P	Wood Sally	(Joel)		Dis. Nov. 11, 1830
Aug. 8, 1824	P	Wood Lucy	(Elijah Smith)		*
Nov. 13, 1831	P	Wood Jabez			Ex. June 13, 1867
Nov. 13, 1831	P	Wood Lucy	(Eli)		*
April 29, 1835	P	Wood Harriet			*
Aug. 9, 1835	P	Wood Lucy	(Eli)		*
May 12, 1839	L	Woods Deborah	(Warren)		Dis. Sept. 7, 1851
March 22, 1812	L	Woodbury Dea. William C.			Ex. Feb. 9, 1826
July 24, 1814	L	Woodbury Martha			Dis. Sept. 30, 1827
Nov. 8, 1818	P	Woodbury Rebecca			Dis. Sept. 30, 1827

MEMBERS.

Year		Name	(Relation)
1819	L	Seus Sanborn	(Dr. Nathan)
1825	P	Nathan Carter	
1828	P	Jacob Gordon	
1830	P	Mary P. Darling	(Enoch)
"	L	Eunice Ward	(Windsor)
1831	P	Sophronia Bowman	(David Davis)
"	P	Margery Carter	(Nathan)
"	P	Dea. Horace Childs	
"	P	Susan C. Cogswell	(Jonathan)
"	P	Hannah Hathorn	(John, jr.)
"	P	Lucy Morrill	(Ephraim, jr.)
"	P	Irene Patten	
"	P	John Peters	
"	P	Avaline Rice	(J. Heath Colby)
"	P	Almary Wadsworth	(Barak Colby)
"	P	John Whitcomb	
"	P	Lydia Whitcomb	
"	L	Sarah Wilkins	(James)
"	P	Rev. William Wood	
"	P	Martha Wood	(Harris Campbell)
1832	P	Zilpha Barnes	
"	P	Warren S. Childs	
"	P	Carlos Childs	
"	P	Barak Colby	
"	P	Dea. Worcester Hathorn	
"	P	Lucinda G. Proctor	(John Proctor / Joseph Thompson)
"	P	Rebecca Ramsdell	
1833	L	Mary L. N. Connor	(Abel)
"	P	Zebulon Foster, jr.	
"	P	Sally Goss	(Luther)
"	P	Gilbert Pillsbury	
"	P	Grizzy D. Rice	(Willard)
"	P	Lucinda Ring	(Benjamin)
1834	P	Polly C. Barnes	(Harry)
"	L	Washington Berry	
"	L	Maria Berry	
"	P	Anna Pillsbury	(Dea. Oliver)
1835	P	Daniel Cogswell	
"	P	A. Whitney Connor	
"	P	Elvira Connor	(J. G. M. Foss)
"	P	Mary J. Darling	(J. Kimball Connor)
"	P	Mary Darling	(Jonas Wallace)
"	P	Henrietta M. Gould	(Charles French)
"	P	Prudence H. Mirick	
"	P	Abigail Newton	

1835	P	Harriet N. Pillsbury	(Nahum Newton)
"	P	Susan E. Smith	(Dr. David O. Collins)
"	P	Sarah Jane Tennant	(Peter N. Peterson)
"	P	Jane W. Wilson	(Worcester Goss)
1836	L	Enoch L. Childs	
"	L	Maria Connor	(William)
1838	P	Harry Barnes	
"	P	Matilda R. S. Childs	(Dea. Horace)
"	P	J. Kimball Connor	
"	P	Esther E. Sargent	(William)
1840	L	Sarah Childs	(Warren S.)
"	L	Mary L. Childs	(Asa Whitney)
1843	P	Worcester Carter	
"	P	A. D. L. F. Connor	
"	L	Susan Moore	(Thomas Wallace / William Moore)
"	P	Rial Mirick	
"	P	Almira Whitcomb	(Dexter)
"	P	Elizabeth S. Whitcomb	
1844	P	Oliver C. Fisher	
"	P	Laura W. Gordon	(Benjamin Clark)
"	L	Sarah A. Morrill	(Ephraim 3d)
"	L	Julia Wood	(Dexter)
"	P	Edna Dean Proctor	
1846	L	Elizabeth Mirick	
1847	L	Harriet N. Connor	(A. Whitney)
1849	P	Susan Mirick	(Rial)
"	P	Thomas L. Sanborn	
1851	L	Rev. J. M. R. Eaton	
"	L	Harriet D. Eaton	
1853	P	Eliza M. Peters	(Levi Newton)
"	P	Livonia Smith	(George Woods)
1854	L	Eliza A. Foster	(Zebulon Jr.)
1855	P	Fidelia H. Carter	(Worcester)
"	P	Sarah M. Cogswell	(Josiah Morse Jr.)
"	P	Lizzie B. Wallace	
"	P	Robert C. Hale	
"	P	Abigail E. Hale	
1856	L	Mary S. Peters	(John)
"	L	S. Worcester Morrison	
"	L	Emily V. Morrison	
1857	P	Rebecca H. Cogswell	(Daniel)
"	P	Susan C. Eastman	
"	L	Joseph Matthews	
1858	P	Helen M. Chase	(Daniel Thompson)
"	P	Lucy M. Cogswell	(Gawn Wilkins)
"	P	Isabella Colton	(Martin Greene)
"	P	Helen C. Goss	
"	P	Ella F. Gould	(Amos D.)
"	P	S. Frances Hathorn	
"	P	Lois F. Mirick	(W. W. Gutterson)
"	P	Nahum Newton	
"	P	Henrietta Wilkins	(J. S. Taylor)
"	P	Ellen F. Wood	(Willis Rice)
1859	P	Mary E. Campbell	
1860	L	Mary Ann Flanders	(Gould)
1861	L	E. Maria Cogswell	(Washington)
"	L	Abigail Colby	(Dea. Nehemiah)
"	L	Sarah M. Colby	(Dr. P. H. Wheeler)
"	L	Lucy S. Connor	(A. D. La Fayette)
"	L	Harriet A. Scribner	(Gilman)
1862	P	Letitia Colby	
"	L	Orpah L. C. Eastman	(George)

1862	L	Sarah A. French	
"	P	S. Anna Hall	
1863	L	Martha D. Gordon	(Francis)
"	P	Malvina M. Matthews	(Norman)
1864	L	Lucy M. Campbell	
"	P	Richard L. Childs	
"	P	Mary A. Childs	
"	P	Frances J. Goss	
"	P	Ephraim P. Goss	
"	P	Lizzie M. Goss	(Fitz Edward Cogswell)
"	P	Thomas L. Brown	
1865	P	Franklin E. Colby	
"	L	S. Frances Gutterson	(John)
1866	L	Mary A. Taylor	
"	L	Sophia Barnes	(Almon Stiles)
1867	L	Mary Felch	(Warren)
"	L	Sarah A. D. Hussey	(Paul)
"	L	Daniel Putney	
"	L	Jenny Wood	(Elisha)
1868	P	Edna F. Connor	
"	P	Helen J. Eastman	
1869	L	Ellen Colby	(Franklin E.)
1870	P	Levi S. Connor	
"	P	Horace Gibson }	
"	P	Mary W. Gibson }	
"	P	Elizabeth H. Gove	(James)
"	P	John Gutterson	
"	P	Louisa B. Howe	
1870	P	Sarah W. Howe	(Rufus)
"	L	Rev. S. S. Morrill }	
"	L	Ellen B. Morrill }	
"	P	Susan L. Rice,	
"	P	Hannah B. Whitney,	(Frederick)
"	P	Annette Jones,	
1871	L	Mary F. Cogswell,	(George)
1872	L	Dr. L. W. Peabody	
"	L	Louisa L. K. Peabody }	
"	L	Sarah M. Peabody	
"	L	Maria A. Peabody	
"	L	Elisha Rice }	
"	L	Ann E. Rice }	
"	L	Hannah E. Smith	
"	P	Susan E. Towle	(Gardiner S.)
"	P	Martha K. Ordway	(Joshua)

SUMMARY.

Number of Pastors,	7
Number of Deacons,	11
Number of original Members,	9
Whole number of Members,	541
Number removed by Dismission,	145
Number removed by Excommunication,	38
Number removed by Death,	207
Present Membership,	151

www.ingramcontent.com/pod-product-compliance
Lightning Source LLC
Chambersburg PA
CBHW020157170426
43199CB00010B/1083